COACHING FOOTBALL'S
3-3-5 DEFENSE

Leo Hand and Rick Molina

ISBN: 1-58518-918-9
Library of Congress Control Number: 2004114027
Book layout and diagrams: Deborah Oldenburg
Cover design: Jeanne Hamilton
Front cover photo: Getty Images

Coaches Choice
P.O. Box 1828
Monterey, CA 93942
www.coacheschoice.com

Dedication

For Mary, Michael, David, and Raina.
L.H.

For my wife and kids, without their patience and understanding,
my goals and dreams would not have been possible.

R.M.

Acknowledgments

Thanks to all of the young coaches whose enthusiasm and
optimism constantly assure an old man that the greatest game of all will
continue to evolve and improve in the future. Additional thanks are extended
to Dr. James Peterson who gave me the opportunity to write this book,
to Allan Sepkowitz who gave me the opportunity to coach at Andress High School,
and also to two of my mentors Jim Murphy and John Robinson.

– L.H.

Thanks to my parents, for believing in me and allowing me
to pursue my goals and dreams.

Thanks to Bill Birkhead, for allowing my coaching career
to get started at Burges High School.

Thanks to Charlie Bailey and his staff at UTEP 1996-1999,
for giving me the opportunity to play the sport I love the most.

Thanks to Troy Reffett, for giving me valuable information
in life and on the football field.

Thanks to Howard Wells and Ron Dentinger, for giving me the chance
to coach at El Paso High School.

Thanks to all of the people with whom I have had the privilege to coach,
and to all the kids whom I had the privilege to coach.

– R.M.

Contents

Passion

Standing on Mexican sand,
watching an amber sun
slowly slide down a crimson sky
into Pacific waters, and
realizing that creation itself
is an ongoing act of passion.

Passion.
The mother of art and poetry.
The father of math and science.
The fire in love.
The lava in a volcano.
The force in a tornado.
The red in a rose.
The jet that
Beiderbecke, Beethoven, and Bach
used to soar to the stars.

Passion.
Without it,
there'd be no itinerate preachers
dying on crosses.
There'd be no Black men
standing in front of the Washington Monument
talking about their dreams.
There'd be no deaf composers
creating the world's greatest symphonies.
There'd be no healthy young doctors
risking death by injecting weakened germs
of deadly diseases into their own bodies.
There'd be no Italian-Americans
pacing the sidelines
and planting seeds of greatness
in Green Bay, Wisconsin.
There'd be no shriveled up old women
easing the pain of death and suffering
in the city of Calcutta.

Passion.
Without it,
there'd be nothing,
nothing at all.

Preface

During the 1970s, John Robinson was head coach at USC. Coach Robinson and his outstanding staff were always extremely cordial and accommodating to high school coaches. They would let high school coaches come right onto the practice field and observe everything and anything that they desired. Being a young ambitious high school coach at that time, I really took advantage of this great opportunity.

One of the things that really fascinated me about Coach Robinson's defense was a variation of the triple stack that he was using. During Coach Robinson's tenure at USC, I rarely missed any of his spring practices and tried learned everything that I could about the triple stack. Through the years, this defense has become my passion; at almost every school that I have coached, I have tried to incorporate the defense into our system. The triple stack has proven to be a great panacea, getting me out of countless defensive dilemmas for more than thirty years.

The modern 3-3-5 is the grandchild of the triple stack. All across the nation, many high school and college coaches have either adopted it as their staple defense, or they are frantically seeking information about it. Like all grandchildren, the modern 3-3-5 still has some growing up to do. Much of what Coach Robinson was doing with the defense back in the '70s has yet to be incorporated into the modern version. Hopefully, this book will fill that void.

It has been a great joy and pleasure to be given the opportunity to write this book, and to share some of the ideas about the triple stack that I have acquired during the past three decades. It has also been an honor to work with my co-author, Rick Molina, who I believe is the finest defensive backfield coach in the state of Texas.

– L.H.

Introduction

What Is in This Book for You

- A complete playbook for the 3-3-5 defense, capable of dealing with all of the problems that may confront a modern defense.
- All of the terminology necessary to install the entire system.
- Detailed explanations and illustrations of how to stop football's most explosive running plays with the 3-3-5 defense.
- The assignments and techniques necessary to implement the most effective pass coverages (both man and zone) versus the modern passing game.
- A complete stunt package that complements and enhances each pass coverage.
- An elucidation of the specific techniques necessary to stop football's most commonly used individual pass routes.
- An impenetrable 3-3-5 goal line package.
- Suggestions on how to organize a 3-3-5 practice schedule.

Following are explanations of terms that will constantly be referred to throughout the text:

- *Strongside/weakside*: The strongside is toward the tight end and the weakside is toward the split end. Strong defenders (example: strong tackle) are aligned on the tight end side, and weak defenders are aligned on the split end side.

- *Gap responsibilities* will be given letter designations as shown in Diagram Intro-1.

- The *alignment numbering system* is shown in Diagram Intro-2.

- Diagram Intro-3 illustrates receiver numbers and formation names.

Diagram Intro-1

Diagram Intro-2

The following are the names that will be given to various offensive formations:

- **Pro**–*Intro 3-A* (standard flanker/split end, 2-back set).
- **Twin**–*Intro 3-B* (split end and flanker are aligned on the same side of the formation).
- **Aceback**–*Intro 3-C and 3-B* (any offensive set with only one back in the backfield).
- **Doubles**–*Intro 3-C* (a balanced aceback formation with two receivers on both sides of the center).
- **Trips**–*Intro 3-D* (an unbalanced aceback formation with three receivers on one side of the center and one receiver on the other side).
- **Empty**–*Intro 3-E* (an offensive formations with only the quarterback in the backfield).
- **Shotgun**–*Intro 3-E* (an offensive formation in which the quarterback is not positioned under the center but is catching the back directly from the center. Can also be used with any of the other illustrated formations—not just empty).

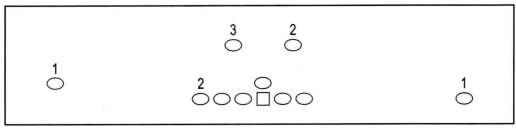

Diagram Intro-3a

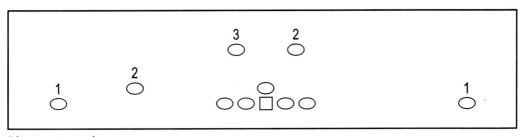

Diagram Intro-3b

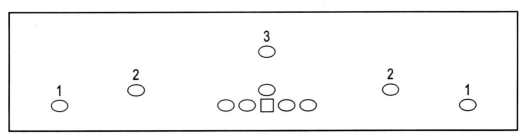

Diagram Intro-3c

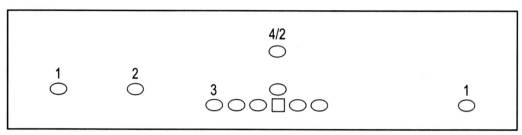

Diagram Intro-3d

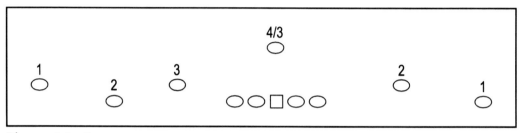

Diagram Intro-3e

Personnel Designations

Because a defense needs to be able to match up its personnel with the offensive personnel that are on the field, we also refer to formations according to the type of personnel that are on the field. First, we account for the number of running backs (zero, one, two, or three); then, we account for the number of tight ends (one or two). Using this system, the formations illustrated in *Intro 3-A, B, C, D, and E* are referred to as follows:

- **Pro**–21 Personnel.
- **Twin**–20 Personnel.
- **Aceback Doubles**–10 Personnel.
- **Aceback Trips**–11 Personnel.
- **Empty Shotgun**–Zero Personnel.

1

Overview of the 3-3-5

The 3-3-5 defense is a coadunation of old school wisdom and modern innovation. The stacking of a linebacker behind a defensive lineman became popular in professional football in the1930s when the 5-3 defense reigned as the standard defense. The concept surfaced again in the NFL when Hank Stram eliminated the two defensive ends from the old 5-3 scheme and replaced them with a linebacker and a defensive back. Stram's Kansas City triple stack was an innovation that helped the Chiefs win Super Bowl IV. The Kansas City defense is very similar to the modern 3-3-5, but because so many offenses now employ spread formations that feature 10 or zero personnel, many coaches have added a fifth defensive back into their triple stack alignment. Although the fifth defensive back is extremely effective against modern spread offenses, coaches—particularly at the high school level—will frequently find themselves lining up against opponents who are still playing *smash-mouth* football. Against such opponents, the fifth (and sometimes even the fourth) defensive back may have to be replaced with a linebacker who is more suited for stopping the run.

The Base Defense

Diagram 1-1 illustrates three variations of a 3-3-5 alignment versus a standard pro formation (see Diagrams 1-1A, B, and C) and one variation against an aceback formation (see Diagram 1-1D). Note that the defensive ends are aligned in a 5 technique and the tandem linebackers are not stacked directly behind the ends. The reason for choosing this alignment rather than the popular stacked-6 alignment is because it enables the ends and tandems to employ a *tango read* technique, which makes the defense extremely sound versus any option play. The stacked-6, on the other hand, is vulnerable to the option. It should also be mentioned that the end/tandem alignment does not affect the ability to slant, stunt, or accomplish anything of which the stacked-6 is capable. Also note that the Stud is frequently aligned in a 9 technique. Although the loose 8 technique is ideal most of the time, some offensive schemes will necessitate the use of a 9 technique. The 9 technique becomes necessary when an offense uses their tight end to crack on the strong tandem and nullify the *tango read* technique.

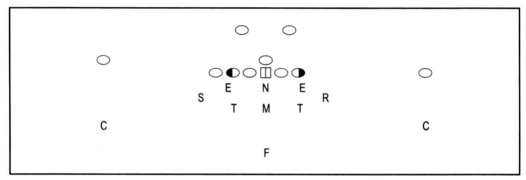

Diagram 1-1a

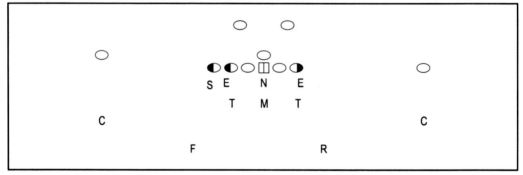

Diagram 1-1b

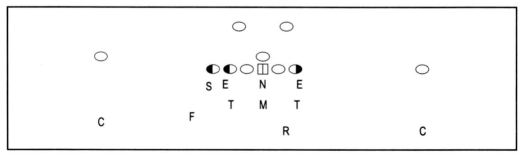

Diagram 1-1c

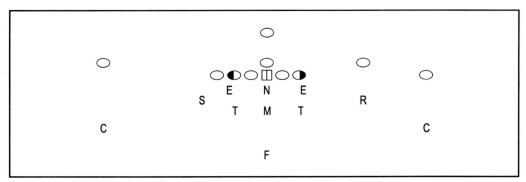

Diagram 1-1d

Stud

This player is either a linebacker or a fifth defensive back. Hopefully he is a hybrid who can not only defeat the block of a big tight end or fullback and effectively shut down an opponent's power running game, but who can also leave the box and cover a swift wide receiver. Stud will line up in either a 9 or an 8 technique. When a team is not blessed with a hybrid, the following guidelines are recommended:

- Use a defensive back versus 10, 20, 11, or 12 personnel.
- Use a defensive back in an obvious passing situation versus any type of personnel.
- Use a defensive back when you plan to blitz Stud from the edge.
- Use a linebacker in all other situations.

Strong and Weak End

Both ends play a 5 technique, employing a *tango* technique with the tandem linebacker. When employing this technique, the end will react to the movement of the offensive tackle. If the offensive tackle blocks inside, the end will jam the tackle and close the B gap. When the tackle blocks the end, he will defeat the tackle's block and secure the C gap. The end should be a strong, physical player who is capable of pressuring and containing the quarterback.

Nose

The Nose plays a 0 technique. He is sometimes asked to control both A gaps, but much of the time he will slant into a specific gap. Because the Nose has a linebacker stacked directly behind him and two other linebackers in his immediate vicinity, he does not have to be as talented in the 3-3-5 scheme as he would have to be in many other schemes. It is imperative, however, that the Nose is physical enough to hold his ground and not get driven backwards.

Rover

The Rover is primarily a defensive back. Versus 22 personnel, a linebacker may have to be substituted for this player. Versus a standard pro formation, Rover will line up in one of the three positions illustrated in Diagrams 1-1A, B, or C. Versus 11, 12, or 10 personnel, he will adjust to the extra receiver and either cover the receiver, or drop to a specific zone. Rover must be a very versatile player with a wide range of skills.

Mike

This defender is the toughest, most physical linebacker. Mike will line up directly behind the Nose. He must be a leader, possess good instincts, and have an intense desire to not only make the tackle, but also to punish the ballcarrier. He is a downhill runner who must quickly plug the B gaps and tackle the ballcarrier from an inside-out position.

Strong and Weak Tandems

Some coaches may wish to designate these players as *right* and *left* rather than flip-flopping them *strong* and *weak*. If so, an additional strength designation must be made as it is recognized (necessary to orchestrate a sophisticated stunt game). The tandems will line up inside shade of the offensive tackles and read the triangle formed by the guard, tackle, and near back. They will employ a *tango* technique with the defensive ends. If the offensive tackle blocks the defensive end, the tandem will plug the B gap; if the offensive tackle blocks inside, the tandem will scrape to the C gap.

Free Safety

This defender will line up in any of the three positions illustrated in Diagram 1-1. The free safety must possess the speed, range, and instincts to play center field. He must also have the physical toughness to provide adequate run support.

Field Corner

The field corner is your team's best cover player. He must cover the #1 receiver aligned toward the wide side of the field with no help from the free safety. When the ball is in the middle of the field, he will cover your opponent's best receiver.

Boundary Corner

He will line up to the short side of the field and cover #1. This player will usually receive help from the free safety. He should be the second-best coverage player on the defense.

Advantages of the 3-3-5

- It is new and many coaches are not really sure how to block it and effectively game-plan against it.
- It is extremely flexible. Nickel-dime substitutions can easily be made without disrupting the overall scheme, which enables the defense to automatically adapt itself to any type of offensive personnel that is on the field.
- The defense is an eight-man front, which gives it an advantage against the run. Despite this strength, the defense always has four or five defensive backs on the field, which also makes it a great pass defense.
- The triple stack frequently results in one of the stacked linebackers ending up unblocked.
- The defense is sound versus the option; many eight-man fronts are not.
- Pass coverages are easily disguised.
- The defense is conducive to multiple coverages.
- An explosive stunt package can easily be installed into the system.

3-3-5 Defensive Philosophy

You are not counter punchers. You do not react; you attack. You are a rowdy bunch with an attitude—a bad attitude. You are the aggressors, the pursuers, the raiders, and the invaders. To be a member of this elite group, a man must be a warrior. To be a warrior, he must be willing to *sell out* every single play, to play with reckless abandon, to hold nothing back. To be a warrior, a man must be mentally and physically tough. He must be totally unselfish; he must be disciplined. He must take it upon himself to personally take the ball away from the offense. The 3-3-5 defensive philosophy is to be multiple, to be different, to disguise, and to attack.

To Be Multiple

You want to present the offense with many different fronts and coverages. You want the offense to spend a lot of time trying to prepare for you, and you want to burden them mentally. You will not find a *best* front or coverage versus a single offensive formation or tactic. Despite the defense's physical ability, a good offense will eventually pick apart the defense if it attempts to sit in a single defense all evening.

To Be Different

Geronimo did not fight like the Cavalry. His strategy and tactics kept them in a constant state of confusion; consequently, it took one-third of the United States Cavalry (5,000+

men) to force Geronimo and his band of *34* Chiricahua renegades to surrender. You want to fight like Geronimo. You want to be different, more creative, more intelligent, and better than any other defense in America.

To Disguise

Force each of your opponents to have to deal with both a pre-snap and post-snap read. Show one *look* before the ball is snapped, and then do something entirely different after the snap. Stem and shift while the quarterback is calling signals. Never allow a physically superior opponent the luxury of lining up, winding up, and kicking *gluteus maximus*. Keep your opponents on their heels. You want them constantly guessing about what you are going to do.

To Attack

- *The quarterback*: Sack the quarterback. Force him to throw off-balance, and to make bad decisions and hurried throws. Intimidate the quarterback and extinguish his enthusiasm, poise, and confidence.
- *Receivers*: Taunt and torment them; knock them around. Disrupt their timing by forcing them to run collision courses, and then knock them out should they ever be lucky enough to catch the ball.
- *Running backs*: Pursue relentlessly. Stalk and swarm ballcarriers like a pack of hungry wolves. Pillage their enthusiasm by constantly pounding and punishing them.
- *Offensive linemen*: Overload their minds with a multitude of fronts, stunts, and line twists. Complicate and confuse their blocking assignments. Curb their aggression by creating havoc.
- *Game plans*: Take away what your opponents do best and force them to do something that they do not want to do. Control the game and force them to play it by your rules.
- *The ball*: It is your ball, not theirs! You must rip it, strip it, recover it, snatch it out of the air, and then score with it.

2

Base Responsibilities of the Front 8

Strong and Weak End

Base Read Technique

Stance and Alignment

Three- or four-point stance, inside foot back. 5 technique: player's inside foot should split the offensive tackle's stance.

Responsibilities

- Run toward: C gap if blocked by the tackle. Squeeze the B gap if the tackle blocks inside.
- Run away: Squeeze B and chase.
- Pass: Contain quarterback.

Keys

- Primary: Tackle, ball movement.
- Secondary: Tight end, near back, pulling linemen.

Important Techniques/Concepts

Defender's target is the tackle's outside shoulder. His first step is with his inside foot. He must maintain outside leverage, secure the C gap, and not get hooked by the tackle. Defender will employ a *tango* technique. If the tackle blocks inside, the end will jam the tackle and secure the B gap, if the tackle tries to hook him, the defender must secure the C gap.

Key Blocks

- Tackle drive block: Defender must read tackle's head, fight pressure, and secure the C gap before pursuing the ball.
- Tackle hook block: Defender must maintain outside leverage, keep his shoulders parallel to the line of scrimmage, and plug the C gap.
- Tackle turn out block: Defender must squeeze the B gap with the tackle's body and look for cutback as he pursues down the line.
- Tackle/tight end double team: Defender must attack the tight end and not get driven back. As a last resort, he should drop his outside hip and roll into and plug the C gap.
- Strong Zone: Defender must play the tackle's block like a hook block.
- Guard blocks inside/tight end cracks: Defender must first jam the tackle, release pressure, and then flatten across the tight end's face.
- Guard blocks inside/no outside pressure: This play is a trap. Defender must immediately squeeze the B gap and attack the pulling guard with an outside forearm. He must spill the play outside.
- Tackle pulls inside: This play is most likely a counter trey. Defender must get in the tackle's hip pocket and follow him to the point of attack.
- Tackle pulls outside: If the tight end cracks on the defender, he must fight outside pressure and flatten across the tight end's face. If the tight end does not crack, the play is either a quick pitch or a trap. The defender must read the backfield action and trap the trapper (if the play is a trap), or pursue the quick pitch flat down the line. If the defender attempts to stop a quick pitch with penetration across the line, he will end up chasing air.
- Tackle pass blocks: Defender must contain the quarterback.

Outside Slant Technique

Stance and Alignment

Three- or four-point stance. 5 technique.

Responsibilities

- Run: C gap.
- Pass: Contain the quarterback if Stud is involved in coverage.

Keys

- Primary: Tackle.
- Secondary: Tight end/near back.

Important Concepts/Techniques

Defender lead steps with near foot and then brings back foot through to avoid tackle's block. He will rip backside forearm through with movement of back foot and penetrate with his inside hip almost perpendicular to the line. Defender will square up quickly and be ready to move in either direction. He will anticipate the tight end's block if aligned on strongside, and the near back's block if aligned on weakside.

Key Blocks

- Tackle drive blocks defender: Defender will rip through the tackle's head, turn the tackle's shoulders, and control the C gap. If play is toward his slant, he will flatten out and go to the ball. If play is away from his slant and he has gained penetration, he will go behind the tackle. If he has not gained penetration, he will come across the tackle's face.
- Tackle/guard zone away from defender's slant: Defender will gain quick penetration and flatten back in the opposite direction.
- Tackle/guard zone toward defender's slant: Defender will rip through the tackle's head and prevent the tackle from releasing to next level. Defender will avoid the guard's block, plug the C gap, and bounce play outside.
- Tackle/end double-team: Defender will attack the tight end and try to flatten across his face. It is vital that he does not get driven back.
- Tackle blocks, inside-defender is left unblocked: Defender must stop immediately! He will flatten back in opposite direction. The point of attack is either away, or he is being trapped. If the point of attack is away, he will chase as deep as the ball; if trapped, the defender will trap the trapper with his outside arm and bounce the play outside.

Inside Slant Technique

Stance and Alignment

Three- or four-point stance. 5 technique.

Responsibilities

- Run: B gap.
- Pass: Penetrate and rush through the B gap.

Keys

- Primary: Guard.
- Secondary: Tackle.

Important Concepts/Techniques

Defender lead steps with his near foot and then brings his back foot through to avoid tackle's block. He will rip his backside forearm through with movement of his back foot, penetrate with his inside hip almost perpendicular to line, square up quickly, and be ready to move in either direction.

Key Blocks

- Tackle drive blocks defender and guard scoops nose: Defender will rip through the tackle's head, turn the tackle's shoulders, and control the B gap. He will then flatten and go to the ball.
- Tackle/guard zone away from defender's slant: Defender will ricochet off the guard's block and flatten back in opposite direction.
- Tackle/guard zone toward defender's slant: Defender will rip through the tackle's head and quickly penetrate the B gap.
- Guard pulls inside-tackle and tries to cut defender off: Defender will rip through the tackle's head and follow the guard to point of attack.
- Guard blocks inside, defender is left unblocked: The play is a trap. Defender will trap the trapper with his outside arm and bounce the play outside.

Nose

Base Read Technique

Stance and Alignment

Three- or four-point stance. Minimum-to-no stagger of the feet. Zero technique, nose-to-nose with the center.

Responsibilities

- Run: Playside A gap.
- Pass: Rush either A gap.

Keys

- Primary: Center, ball movement.
- Secondary: Both guards.

Important Techniques/Concepts

- Target: Center's facemask.
- Crush technique: Defender will attack the center with his hands, inside lockout. He will take a short jab step in the direction of the play, keep his shoulders square to the line of scrimmage, and control both A gaps. It is vital that he remembers that pulling guards indicate the point of attack.
- Prevent the scoop: It is absolutely imperative that Nose is able to prevent the center and the backside guard from scoop blocking him and the Mike linebacker. If the Nose cannot prevent the center from working to the second level and blocking Mike, the 3-3-5 will become immediately ineffective.

Key Blocks

- Center drive block: Defender will knock the center back. He will stay square, locate the ball, and pursue from an inside-out position.
- Center/guard double-team: Defender will attack the guard, stay low, and not get driven back. As a last resort, he will drop his outside hip and roll into and plug the A gap.
- Center hook block: Defender will control the center's outside shoulder. He will keep his shoulders parallel to the line of scrimmage and pursue the ball from an inside-out position. It is vital that the Nose does not get hooked.
- Guard/center zone-blocking scheme: Defender will play the center's block like a hook block. It is vital that he jams the center and prevents the center from releasing to the next level to block a linebacker.

- Center blocks away/down block by guard: Defender releases from the center and controls the outside shoulder of the guard.
- Pass: Defender will rush either A gap.

Slant Technique

Stance and Alignment

Same as read technique.

Responsibilities

- Run: A gap in the direction of his slant.
- Pass: Rush quarterback through the A gap in direction of his slant.

Keys

- Primary: Ball movement; guard in direction of his slant.
- Secondary: Center

Important Concepts/Techniques

Defender lead steps with his near foot and then brings his back foot through to avoid the center's block. He will rip his backside forearm through with movement of his back foot, penetrate with his inside hip almost perpendicular to line, and square up quickly and be ready to move in either direction.

Key Blocks

- Center blocks defender: Defender rips through the center's head, turns the center's shoulders, and controls the A gap. If play is toward his slant, he will flatten out and go to the ball; if play is away from his slant and he has gained penetration, defender will go around the center. If he has not gained penetration, he will come across the center's face.
- Center/guard zone away from defender's slant: Defender will ricochet off the guard's block and flatten back in the opposite direction.
- Center/guard zone toward defender's slant: Defender will rip through the center's head and prevent the center from releasing to next level. He will avoid the guard's block and plug the A gap before pursuing down the line.
- Guard pulls in direction of defender's slant: Defender will rip through the center's head and follow the guard to the point of attack.

- Guard pulls in opposite direction of defender's slant: Center will block the defender. If he has gained penetration, the defender will go behind the center; if he has not gained penetration, he will come across the center's face.
- Guard/center double-team toward defender's slant: Defender will attack the guard and try to flatten across his face. It is vital that the defender does not get driven back.
- Guard/center double-team away from defender's slant: Defender will work for penetration and try to go behind the center's block.

Stud and Rover

8 Technique

Stance and Alignment

Two-point stance, inside foot back in a loose 8 technique. Depending upon the down and distance situation and offensive tendency, Stud and Rover may line up anywhere from two to five yards deep/outside of the tight end when playing an 8 technique.

Responsibilities

- Run toward: Come up quickly and secure the D gap.
- Run away: Check the tight end first, and then pursue.
- Pass: Depends upon stunt and coverage.

Keys

- Primary: Tight end (if there is one).
- Secondary: Near back, pulling linemen.

Important Techniques

Defender is both a linebacker and defensive back. He must be able to instantly read and react to the tight end's movements (near back if no tight end is present). It is vital that the defender keeps his shoulders parallel to the line of scrimmage and his outside leg back and unblocked. He will defeat the tight end's block with a hand shiver and use a forearm rip to defeat the block of a pulling lineman or near back. It is important that the defender's pad level is lower than that of the blocker, and that the defender meets all blockers as near to the line of scrimmage as possible. If he penetrates too deeply, he may create a funnel for the ballcarrier. When the tight end blocks inside, the defender must come up quickly, constrict the C gap, and secure the D gap. When the tight end releases, the defender must simultaneously read the near back. If the near back's movements indicate run, the defender must control the tight end's outside shoulder and contain the run; if the play is pass, his technique will vary depending upon the coverage.

Key Blocks

- Tight end blocks inside; near back kick-out: This block is an off-tackle play. Defender must fill tight to the tight end's block and seal off any inside seams. He must attack the blocker with an inside forearm and maintain outside leverage.
- Tight end blocks inside; near back hook blocks: This block is a sweep. Defender must keep his shoulders parallel to line of scrimmage and maintain outside leverage. He must control the blocker's outside shoulder and force the ballcarrier inside or wide and deep.
- Tight end blocks defender or releases; near back blocks inside: The play could be a run or play-action pass. Defender must jam the tight end. If the tight end's release indicates pass, the defender must cover the tight end or drop to his designated zone. If the tight end blocks the defender, he must squeeze the play inside, maintain outside leverage, and expect the ballcarrier to break play outside.
- Tight end reaches defender; near back leads outside: The play is a sweep. Defender must beat the tight end's block and *blow the play up* in backfield or string it to the sidelines.
- Tight end releases; flow away: Defender must first check the tight end for throwback and then pursue.
- Tight end releases; near back pass blocks: The play is a pass. Defender must cover the tight end or release to his designated zone.

9 Technique

Stance and Alignment

Two-point stance. Feet parallel or slight stagger of inside foot. 9 technique with defender's inside foot slightly inside of the tight end's outside foot.

Responsibilities

- Run toward: D gap.
- Run away: Sink, check the tight end for throwback, and then pursue.
- Pass: Depends upon stunt and coverage.

Keys

- Primary: Tight end.
- Secondary: Near back, pulling linemen, the ball.

Important Techniques

Defender must step with inside foot and jam the tight end. He must maintain outside leverage and not get driven back or hooked. He will attack the tight end with his hands and use a forearm rip when taking on a running back or pulling lineman. When dealing with a cut block, the defender must use his hands, sprawl, and immediately ricochet off the ground.

Key Blocks

- Tight end hook block defender: He will immediately get his hands on the tight end and lock him out. He must control the tight end's outside shoulder and secure the D gap.
- Tight end turn out block; strongside run in the B or C gap: Defender will create a stalemate and squeeze the C gap with the tight end's body while maintaining outside leverage on the ball.
- Tight end releases; near back kick-out block: As the defender jams tight end, he must see near back out of his periphery. Defender must close back inside and constrict the C gap. He will attack the blocker with an inside forearm. It is important that the defender does not penetrate across the line of scrimmage and create an alley for the ballcarrier.
- Tight end releases; flow away: Defender will sink, check the tight end for throwback, and then pursue the ball.
- Tight end blocks inside: Defender must jam the tight end and squeeze the C gap. He will then attack the blocker (near back or pulling lineman) with an inside forearm rip.
- Tight end releases; pass: Depends upon stunt and coverage.

Crash Technique

Stance and Alignment

Defender creeps toward the line during cadence and rush from the edge. His aiming point is the junction of the near back's neck and shoulders. If executed from a 9 technique, the defender will widen to a point at least one yard outside of the tight end during cadence and then rush from the edge at the snap of the ball.

Responsibilities

- Run toward: Contain.
- Run away: Chase.
- Pass: Contain the quarterback.

Keys

- Primary: Near back.
- Secondary: Ball.

Important Techniques/Concepts

Defender's target is the junction of the near back's neck and shoulders. At the snap, he will crash toward this landmark, maintain outside leverage, and attack all blockers with an inside forearm rip.

Key Blocks

- Near back kick-out block: Defender will squeeze the play inside. He will attack the blocker with an inside forearm rip and maintain the ability to react outside.
- Near back hook block: Defender will force the play wide and deep. He will attack the blocker with an inside forearm rip, keep the ballcarrier deeper than himself, and then ricochet off the blocker as the ballcarrier bounces the play outside.
- Near back blocks inside: Defender will redirect his course as he mirrors the path of the near back. He will squeeze play inside, maintain outside leverage on the ball, and be prepared for the ballcarrier to bounce outside.
- Tight end kick-out block: Defender will attack the tight end with an inside forearm rip and use the tight end's body to restrict the C gap. He will maintain outside leverage on the ball and expect the play to bounce outside.
- Flow away: Defender will chase the pay as deep as the ball. He will check for counter and reverse.
- Near back pass blocks: Defender will contain the quarterback.

Tandem Linebackers

Base Read Technique

Stance and Alignment

Defender aligns his outside foot opposite the inside foot of the offensive tackle. His depth will vary depending upon the down and distance and offensive tendency. Normal depth is five yards from the line of scrimmage.

Responsibilities

- Run toward: B gap if the offensive tackle blocks the end. C gap if the offensive tackle blocks inside.
- Run away: Attack the line of scrimmage *downhill* and pursue ball from an inside-out position.
- Pass: Depends upon coverage.

Keys

Keys the near back through the offensive tackle and guard.

Important Techniques/Concepts

Defender keeps his shoulders parallel to the line of scrimmage, pursues the ball from an inside-out position, and attacks blockers with a forearm rip technique.

Key Blocks

- Tackle attempts to block the defender: Defender must shuffle outside and avoid the tackle's block. He will then work downhill, secure the C gap, and pursue the ball from an inside-out position.
- Tackle blocks the end (inside play): Defender must immediately plug the B gap. He will expect to be blocked by the offensive guard or near back. He will attack either blocker with an inside forearm rip.
- Tackle blocks the end (outside play): Defender must first secure the B gap. In all probability the offensive guard will block him. He will attack the guard with an inside forearm rip and then pursue the ball from an inside-out position.
- *Down-Down* Call from Stud: Whenever the tight end blocks inside, Stud will give the defender a *down-down* call. Upon hearing this call the defender must immediately shuffle outside and react to the tight end's block. If the tight end is double-teaming the defensive end, the tandem linebacker will scrape outside and secure the D gap

(Stud will be closing inside tight to the double team). If the tight end is attempting to block the tandem linebacker, the linebacker will rip through the tight end's face and secure the D gap.

- Tackle-guard pulls inside: This play is most likely a counter trey. Defender must work downhill, secure the B gap (if he sees a window, he will take it and pursue along the heel line). If no window exists, the defender will pursue from an inside-out position.
- Tackle pass blocks: Defender must contain the quarterback.

Reads and Techniques When End Slants

Stance and Alignment

Same as base read.

Responsibilities

- Run: Plugs the B or C gap depending on the offensive tackle's block and the direction of the end's slant.
- Pass: Depends upon coverage.

Keys

- Primary: Tackle to near back.
- Secondary: Pulling linemen.

Important Techniques

Defender must keep his shoulders parallel to the line and attack blocks as close to the line as possible. Defender should attack blocker's outside shoulder with his outside leg back. He should pursue runs from an inside-out position.

Key Blocks

- End slants outside; tackle blocks end: Defender will fill B gap and attack the blocking guard or near back as close to line as possible. He must maintain outside leverage, bounce the play outside, and then pursue from an inside-out position.
- End slants outside; tackle blocks tandem linebacker: If flow is toward him, the defender will rip through tackle's block with his outside forearm, secure the B gap, and pursue the ball from an inside-out position. If flow is away from him, the defender will avoid tackle's block (or ricochet off it), and pursue the ball from an inside-out position.

- End slants outside; tackle blocks Mike: This play is a trap. Defender must fill the B gap.
- End slants inside; tackle blocks end: Defender must read the near back and backfield flow. If flow is away, the defender will pursue from inside out position checking for cutback; if flow is toward him, he will immediately fill the C gap.
- End slants inside; tackle blocks tandem linebacker: Defender will fill the C gap. He will attack the tackle as close to line as possible, maintain outside leverage, bounce the play outside, and then pursue the ball from an inside-out position.
- End slants inside; tackle blocks Mike: This play is a trap. Defender will fill tight to the defensive end's tail.
- Tight end/tackle double-team end: Defender will fill close to double-team, take on near back or pulling lineman with his inside forearm, maintain outside leverage, and bounce play outside.
- Tight end blocks tandem linebacker: Defender will attack the tight end, rip through the tight end's face, and secure the D gap.
- Pass: Depends upon coverage.

Mike Linebacker

Base Read Technique

Stance and Alignment

Two-point stance, feet parallel. Stack behind the nose three to five yards deep.

Responsibilities

- Run: Defender will come up quickly and plug the B gap.
- Pass: Depends upon coverage.

Keys

- Primary: Backfield flow.
- Secondary: Pulling guards (take precedence).

Important Techniques

Mike is the plugger. He must keep his shoulders parallel to the line and attack the blockers as close to the line as possible. It is important that he attack the blocker's outside shoulder with his outside leg back. Mike is responsible for cutback and should pursue runs from an inside-out position.

Key Blocks

- Flowside guard blocks Mike: He will attack the guard's outside shoulder as close to line as possible, maintain outside leverage, bounce the play outside, and pursue from an inside-out position.
- Flowside guard pulls opposite flow: Mike will immediately reverse direction (if he has been fooled by flow) and plug the opposite B gap in the direction of the guard's pull.
- Flowside tackle blocks Mike: Mike will control the tackle's outside shoulder and fill outside of his block.
- Flow side guard blocks Nose; near back blocks Mike: The play is an iso. Mike will attack the blocking back's outside shoulder with an inside forearm rip as close to line of scrimmage as possible. He will maintain outside leverage and spill the play outside.
- Pass: Depends upon coverage.

3

Stopping Football's
Most Potent Running Plays
with the 3-3-5 Base Read Front

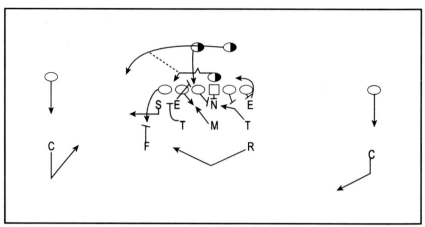

Diagram 3-1

PLAY DESCRIPTION: With this two-back inside veer, the playside offensive tackle blocks Mike.

COACHING POINTS: The *tango* read employed by the playside defensive end and the tandem linebacker is the key to stopping this play. Also, whenever an offense uses a two-back set, the defense can enhance its run support by employing a rotating four-deep secondary.

STUD: As the tight end releases and the defender reads backfield flow, he will sink one-and-a-half yards deep and get his feet moving. He will then *feather* the quarterback. Feathering the quarterback means that the defender will make it appear as though he is covering the quarterback, but once the pitchback gets even with him, the defender must then play the pitch.

STRONG END: Defender must jam the offensive tackle, and then attack the mesh point. It is vital that the defender penetrates the line of scrimmage and tackles the diveback in the backfield, forcing the quarterback to continue to run the option *downhill*.

STRONG TANDEM: As he sees the offensive tackle block inside, the defender must scrape to the C gap and attack the quarterback. If possible, the defender should tackle the quarterback's pitch arm.

NOSE: Defender will plug the playside A gap by attempting to split the double-team. It is imperative that the defender does not lose ground and get driven backwards into the path of pursuing linebackers.

MIKE: Upon reading backfield flow, Mike will plug the B gap and attack the offensive tackle with an outside forearm rip, preventing the cutback and spilling the diveback's course outside.

WEAK END: Defender must defeat the offensive tackle's block and chase the play along the heel line. He must look for cutback, counter, and reverse.

WEAK TANDEM: Upon reading backfield flow, the defender will shuffle two steps parallel to the line and then work downhill. He will then rip through the offensive guard's block and pursue the play from an inside-out position.

ROVER: Upon reading flow, defender will begin to retreat to centerfield. When he is sure that the play is a run, he will play the alley.

FREE SAFETY: Upon reading flow and the tight end's release, defender will attack the tight end's outside shoulder, check for a dump pass, defeat the tight end's block, and then assist in defending the pitch.

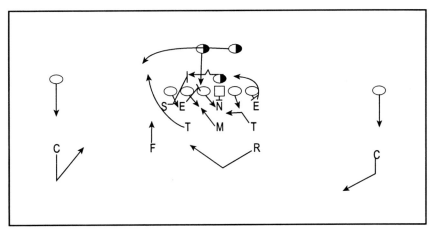

Diagram 3-2

PLAY DESCRIPTION: This play is a two-back inside veer in which the playside offensive tackle blocks Mike and the tight end attempts to wall off the playside tandem linebacker. This offensive tactic is common versus the *tango* technique.

COACHING POINTS: Playing the Stud in a 9 technique and having him jam the tight end and thus preventing the tight end from walling off the tandem linebacker is the key to stopping this play.

STUD: Defender will jam the tight end and prevent him from releasing up field. As he jams the tight end, he will give the tandem linebacker a *down-down* call which will alert the linebacker to scrape to pitch. After riding the tight end down the line, the Stud will tackle the quarterback by attacking his pitch arm.

STRONG END: Defender must jam the offensive tackle and then attack the mesh point. It is vital that the defender penetrates the line of scrimmage and tackles the diveback in the backfield, forcing the quarterback to continue to run the option *downhill*.

STRONG TANDEM: As he sees the offensive tackle block inside, the defender will begin to scrape to the C gap, but as he hears the *down-down* call, he will scrape one gap wider and tackle the pitchback in the backfield.

NOSE: Defender will plug the playside A gap by attempting to split the double-team. It is imperative that the defender does not lose ground and get driven backwards into the path of pursuing linebackers.

MIKE: Upon reading backfield flow, Mike will plug the B gap and attack the offensive tackle with an outside forearm rip, preventing the cutback and spill the diveback's course outside.

WEAK END: Defender must defeat the offensive tackle's block and chase the play along the heel line. He must look for cutback, counter, and reverse.

WEAK TANDEM: Upon reading backfield flow, the defender will shuffle two steps parallel to the line and then work downhill. He will then rip through the offensive guard's block and pursue the play from an inside-out position.

ROVER: Upon reading flow, defender will begin to retreat to centerfield. When he is sure that the play is a run, he will play the alley.

FREE SAFETY: Upon reading flow and the tight end's attempt to release inside, the defender will immediately attack the line of scrimmage. He will play quarterback to pitch.

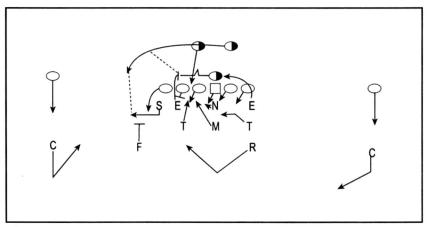

Diagram 3-3

PLAY DESCRIPTION: With this two-back inside veer, the offensive tackle blocks the defensive end.

COACHING POINTS: Again, the *tango* read employed by the play side defensive end and the tandem linebacker is the key to stopping this play.

STUD: As the tight end releases and the defender reads backfield flow, he will sink one-and-a-half yards deep, get his feet moving, and feather the quarterback. He is responsible for pitch.

STRONG END: Defender must aggressively attack the offensive tackle's outside shoulder and work for penetration. He is responsible for tackling the quarterback. It is vital that the defensive end holds his ground and is not driven to the outside because if this were to occur, a running lane would develop for the quarterback.

STRONG TANDEM: As he sees the offensive tackle block the defensive end, the defender must immediately plug the B gap, defeat the offensive guard's block with an inside forearm rip, and tackle the diveback. It is important that the defender maintains an outside leverage relationship with the diveback as he makes the tackle.

NOSE: Defender will jam the center and prevent him from releasing to the next level. He will then plug playside A gap and attack the diveback by pursuing flat down the line of scrimmage.

MIKE: Mike is the *hit-man*. He will attack the diveback from an inside-out position. Since he is unblocked, he should really be able to punish the diveback and convince him that football is not a fun game.

WEAK END: Defender will chase the play along the heel line. He must look for cutback, counter, and reverse. Because he is unblocked, a quick end may be able to tackle the quarterback from behind.

WEAK TANDEM: Upon reading backfield flow, the defender will shuffle two steps parallel to the line and then work downhill. He will then will rip through the offensive guard's block (if the guard releases to the second level) and pursue the play from an inside-out position.

ROVER: Upon reading flow, defender will begin to retreat to centerfield. When he is sure that the play is a run, he will play the alley.

FREE SAFETY: Upon reading flow and the tight end's release, defender will attack the tight end's outside shoulder, check for a dump pass, defeat the tight end's block, and then assist in defending the pitch.

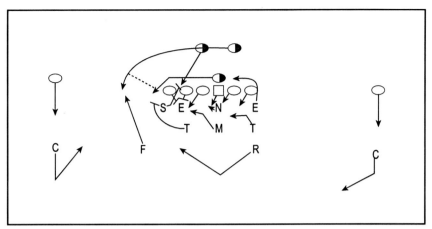

Diagram 3-4

PLAY DESCRIPTION: This play is a two-back outside veer.

COACHING POINTS: The *tango* read and the down-down call are the keys to stopping this play.

STUD: Defender will jam the tight end. He will close tight to the double-team and force a double-team by preventing the tight end from working to the next level. As he jams the tight end, he will give the tandem linebacker a *down-down* call which will alert the linebacker to scrape to quarterback. After riding the tight end down the line, the Stud will tackle the diveback as deep in the backfield as possible.

STRONG END: Defender must aggressively attack the offensive tackle's outside shoulder and work for penetration. As he feels the double-team and hears the *down-down* call, he will drop low and attempt to split the double-team. It is important that the end does not get driven backwards and cut off linebacker pursuit.

STRONG TANDEM: As he sees the offensive tackle block the defensive end, the defender will begin to move forward. As he begins his movement, he will not only hear the *down-down* call but he will also see the wide path of the diveback. Both of these keys will cause the defender to scrape into the D gap and tackle the quarterback.

NOSE: Defender will jam the center and prevent him from releasing to the next level. He will then plug the playside A gap and attack the diveback by pursuing flat down the line of scrimmage.

MIKE: As reads backfield flow, Mike will immediately work downhill, rip through the offensive guard's block and secure the B gap versus cutback.

WEAK END: Defender will chase the play along the heel line. He must look for cutback, counter, and reverse. Because he is unblocked, a quick end may be able to tackle the quarterback from behind.

WEAK TANDEM: Upon reading backfield flow, the defender will shuffle two steps parallel to the line and then work downhill. He will then will rip through the offensive guard's block (if the guard releases to the second level) and pursue the play from an inside-out position.

ROVER: Upon reading flow, defender will begin to retreat to centerfield. When he is sure that the play is a run, he will play the alley.

FREE SAFETY: Upon seeing the double-team and reading flow, the free safety will immediately play the pitchback.

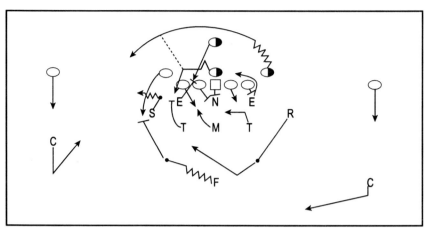

Diagram 3-5

PLAY DESCRIPTION: This play is a flex-bone version of the inside veer.

COACHING POINTS: The 3-3-5 easily adjusts to the flex bone. When the slotback goes into motion, the formation becomes a two-back set and should be dealt with in the same manner as previously described. Versus the flex bone, the 3-3-5 secondary will either play cover 3 or cover 1. When playing either coverage, the secondary will simply rotate when the slotback goes into motion.

STUD: As the motion call is given by Rover, Stud will move to a 9 technique and be prepared to jam the slotback in the event that he tries to wall off the tandem linebacker. As the defender reads the tight end's release and the backfield flow, he will sink and *feather* the quarterback. He is responsible for stopping the pitch.

STRONG END: Defender must jam the offensive tackle and then attack the mesh point. He will penetrate the line of scrimmage and tackles the diveback in the backfield.

STRONG TANDEM: As he sees the offensive tackle block inside, the defender must scrape to the C gap and attack the quarterback.

NOSE: Defender will plug the playside A gap by attempting to split the double-team.

MIKE: Upon reading backfield flow, Mike will plug the B gap and attack the offensive tackle with an outside forearm rip. He will tackle the dive from an inside-out position.

WEAK END: Defender must defeat the offensive tackle's block and chase the play along the heel line. He must look for cutback, counter, and reverse.

WEAK TANDEM: Upon reading backfield flow, the defender will shuffle two steps parallel to the line and then work downhill. He will rip through the offensive guard's block and pursue the play from an inside-out position.

ROVER: Rover is responsible for alerting the defense that the slotback has gone in motion. He will then begin to slowly rotate to his inverted safety position. Versus pass, he will play centerfield. Versus the illustrated run, he will play the alley when he is certain that that play is a run.

FREE SAFETY: Upon hearing Rover's motion call, the defender will move from centerfield to his inverted safety position. If the coverage is man, he will cover the slotback versus pass. If zone, he will drop curl-out versus pass. When he is certain that the play is a run, he will assist in containment no matter what the coverage may be.

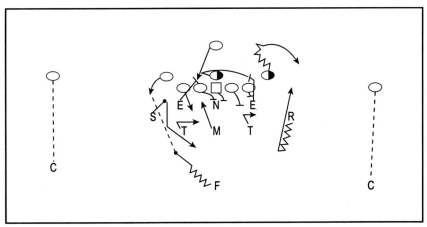

Diagram 3-6

PLAY DESCRIPTION: This play is a flex bone version of the counter option.

COACHING POINTS: Heads-up play by the Rover is vital in stopping this play.

STUD: As Rover gives the motion call, Stud will move to a 9 technique and be prepared to jam the slotback. As he sees the quarterback reverse direction after the fake to the fullback, Stud will immediately begin to fold back and pursue the ball.

STRONG END: Defender must jam the offensive tackle and then attack the mesh point. He will penetrate the line of scrimmage and tackle the diveback in the backfield.

STRONG TANDEM: As he sees the offensive tackle block inside, the defender will begin scrapping to the C gap. As he sees the quarterback reverse direction, the defender will also reverse direction and pursue the ball from an inside-out position.

NOSE: If the Nose reads the blocking pattern correctly, he should not be fooled by the backfield action. He should therefore be able to plug the playside A gap and perhaps even be able to gain penetration through it.

MIKE: Upon reading backfield flow, Mike will plug the B gap and attack the offensive tackle with an outside forearm rip. He will tackle the dive from an inside-out position.

WEAK END: Defender must defeat the offensive tackle's block. As he begins to chase what appears to be Flow away, he should be in great position to immediately attack the quarterback.

WEAK TANDEM: Upon reading backfield flow, the defender will shuffle two steps parallel to the line and then work downhill. As he sees the quarterback reverse direction, he will immediately ricochet off the guard's block and pursue the ball from an inside-out position.

ROVER: Rover is responsible for alerting the defense that the slotback has gone in motion. He will then begin to slowly rotate to his inverted safety position, but as he sees both the slotback and quarterback reverse direction, he will immediately attack the pitch.

FREE SAFETY: Upon hearing Rover's motion call, the defender will move from centerfield to his inverted safety position. As he sees the play develop, he will immediately check the slotback before pursuing the play.

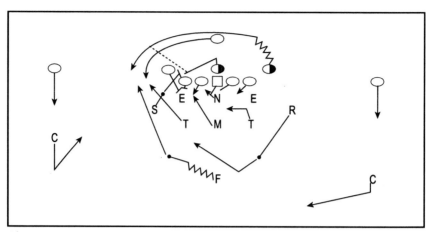

Diagram 3-7

PLAY DESCRIPTION: This play is flex bone lead option.

COACHING POINTS: The key to stopping this play is the *down-down* call by the Stud, and the motion call by the Rover, to alert the secondary to rotate.

STUD: Defender moves to a 9 technique when he hears the Rover's motion call. He will then jam the slotback as he releases inside. As he jams the slotback, Stud will give the tandem linebacker a *down-down* call and then quickly tackle the quarterback.

STRONG END: Defender must aggressively attack the offensive tackle's outside shoulder and work for penetration. As he feels the double-team and hears the *down-down* call, he will drop low and attempt to split the double-team.

STRONG TANDEM: As he sees the offensive tackle block the defensive end, the defender will begin to move forward. As he begins his movement, he will not only hear the *down-down* call, but he will also read backfield flow. Both of these keys will cause the defender to scrape to the D gap. The defender will attack the lead blocker with an inside forearm rip, ricochet off the block, and tackle the pitchback.

NOSE: Defender will jam the center and prevent him from releasing to the next level. He will then plug the playside A gap and pursue flat down the line.

MIKE: As reads backfield flow, Mike will immediately work downhill, rip through the offensive tackle's block, and secure the B gap versus cutback.

WEAK END: Defender will chase the play along the heel line. He must look for cutback, counter, and reverse.

WEAK TANDEM: Upon reading backfield flow, the defender will shuffle two steps parallel to the line and then work downhill. He will then rip through the offensive guard's block (if the guard releases to the second level) and pursue the play from an inside-out position.

ROVER: Rover will alert the defense that the slotback has gone in motion. He will then begin to slowly rotate to his inverted safety position. Versus pass, he will play centerfield; versus the illustrated run, he will play the alley when he is certain that that play is a run.

FREE SAFETY: Upon hearing Rover's motion call, the defender will move from centerfield to his inverted safety position. As he sees the double-team, he will immediately come up and assist in containment.

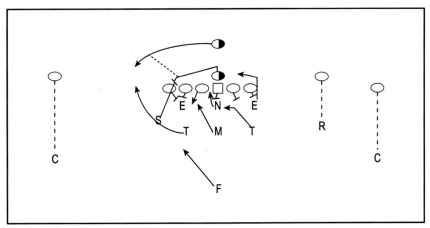

Diagram 3-8

PLAY DESCRIPTION: This play is an aceback speed option.

COACHING POINTS: The keys to stopping this play are the *down-down* call by the Stud, the defensive end forcing a double-team, and the alley support by the free safety.

STUD: Stud will give the tandem linebacker a *down-down* call as he sees the double-team. As he is giving the call, he will close tight to the double-team and force the quarterback to pitch the ball as quickly as possible, using a quick force technique instead of a *feather* technique.

STRONG END: Defender will first attack the offensive tackle's outside shoulder. As he feels the double-team and hears the *down-down* call, he will immediately get his hands on the slotback and prevent him from releasing to the next level. He must force the double-team, stay low and not get driven back.

STRONG TANDEM: The backfield action and the *down-down* call will alert the Stud to scrape outside and tackle the pitch. His depth and the play of the defensive end should prevent the slotback from being able to release to the second level, but should this occur, the tandem linebacker must rip through the slotback's block on his way to the pitch.

NOSE: Defender will jam the center and prevent him from releasing to the next level. He will then plug the playside A gap and pursue flat down the line.

MIKE: As reads backfield flow, Mike will immediately work downhill, rip through the offensive guard's block, and secure the B gap versus cutback.

WEAK END: Defender will chase the play along the heel line. He must look for cutback, counter, and reverse.

WEAK TANDEM: Defender will shuffle two steps parallel to the line and then work downhill. He will rip through the offensive guard's block (if the guard releases to the second level) and pursue the play from an inside-out position.

ROVER: Defender will be involved in coverage.

FREE SAFETY: Defender will provide alley support and check for a tight end delay.

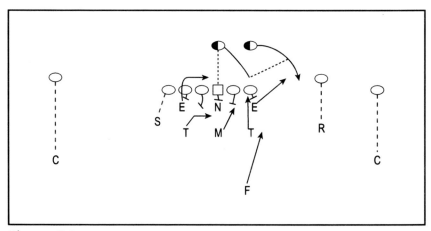

Diagram 3-9

PLAY DESCRIPTION: This weakside speed option is out of the shotgun formation; note that the offensive tackle is attempting to block the defensive end.

COACHING POINTS: The keys to stopping this play are the *tango* technique by the weak end, and tandem and solid alley support by the free safety.

STUD: Defender will be involved in coverage.

STRONG END: Defender will defeat the offensive tackle's block and then chase the play along the heel line. He must look for cutback, counter, and reverse.

STRONG TANDEM: Defender will shuffle two steps parallel to the line and then work downhill. He will rip through the offensive guard's block and pursue the play from an inside-out position.

NOSE: Defender will jam the center and prevent him from releasing to the next level. He will then plug the playside A gap and pursue flat down the line.

MIKE: As reads backfield flow, Mike will immediately work downhill, rip through the offensive guard's block, and secure the B gap versus cutback.

WEAK END: Defender will control the offensive tackle's outside shoulder, gain penetration, and tackle the pitch.

WEAK TANDEM: As he reads backfield flow and the offensive tackle's block, the defender will immediately attack the B gap and tackle the quarterback.

ROVER: Defender will be involved in coverage.

FREE SAFETY: Defender will provide alley support and check for a tight end delay.

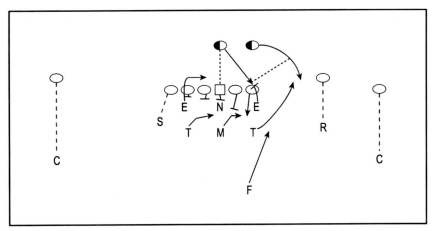

Diagram 3-10

PLAY DESCRIPTION: This weakside speed option is out of the shotgun formation; note that the offensive tackle is attempting to block the tandem linebacker.

COACHING POINTS: The keys to stopping this play are the *tango* technique by the weak end, and tandem and solid alley support by the free safety.

STUD: Defender will be involved in coverage.

STRONG END: Defender will defeat the offensive tackle's block and then chase the play along the heel line. He must look for cutback, counter, and reverse.

STRONG TANDEM: Defender will shuffle two steps parallel to the line and then work downhill. He will rip through the offensive guard's block and pursue the play from an inside-out position.

NOSE: Defender will jam the center and prevent him from releasing to the next level. He will then plug the playside A gap and pursue flat down the line.

MIKE: As reads backfield flow, Mike will immediately work downhill, rip through the offensive guard's block, and secure the B gap versus cutback.

WEAK END: Defender will jam the offensive tackle, give the tandem linebacker a down-down call, and immediately tackle the quarterback. His aiming point will be the quarterback's pitch arm.

WEAK TANDEM: As he reads backfield flow and the offensive tackle's block, the defender will scrape outside and tackle the pitch.

ROVER: Defender will be involved in coverage.

FREE SAFETY: Defender will provide alley support and check for a tight end delay.

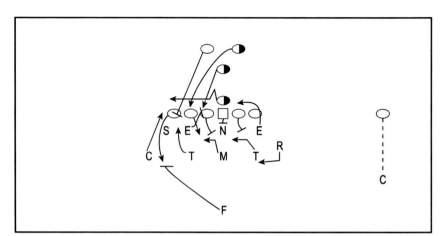

Diagram 3-11

PLAY DESCRIPTION: This play is wishbone belly option. The quarterback is reading the defensive end and will either give the ball to the fullback or the halfback, depending upon the reaction of the defensive end.

COACHING POINTS: When dealing with this (or any other) wishbone option, the defense must deal with the reality of a lead blocker, which requires the defense to get an extra defender to the point of attack. Versus this option, the tandem linebacker is the extra, unblocked defender.

STUD: The defender will line up in a 9 technique and *quick* play—rather than *feather*—any wishbone option. As the tight end releases, Stud will close inside, constrict the C gap, and attack the lead blocker with an inside forearm rip. He will maintain outside leverage as attempts to close the C gap with the lead blocker's body.

STRONG END: Defender must jam the offensive tackle, attack the mesh point, and tackle the fullback as deep in the backfield as possible.

STRONG TANDEM: As he sees the offensive tackle block inside, the defender will scrape—unblocked—to the C gap and tackle the halfback.

NOSE: Defender will attack the center, defeat his block, plug the playside A gap, and pursue flat down the line of scrimmage.

MIKE: Upon reading backfield flow, Mike will plug the B gap and attack the blocker (either the offensive guard or tackle) with an inside forearm rip. He will check for cutback and attempt to spill the play outside.

WEAK END: Defender must defeat the offensive tackle's block and chase the play along the heel line. He must look for cutback, counter, and reverse.

WEAK TANDEM: The defender will shuffle two steps parallel to the line and then work downhill. He will rip through the offensive guard's block and pursue the play from an inside-out position.

ROVER: Defender will fold back and pursue the ball from an inside-out position, checking for counter, reverse, or cutback.

FREE SAFETY: Defender will fill the alley.

CORNER BACK: Defender will jam tight end's release and provide the defense with containment. He is responsible for tackling the quarterback if he should fake to the halfback and keep the ball.

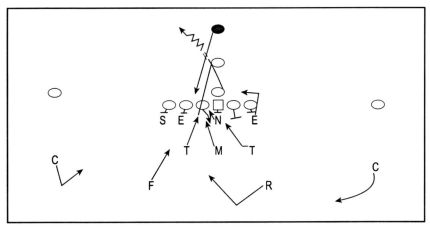

Diagram 3-12

PLAY DESCRIPTION: This play is an I-formation Isolation play.

COACHING POINTS: The offense is in a mathematical disadvantage when attempting to run this play. The technique of the Nose is one of the keys in stopping the play.

STUD: Defender will line up in a 9 technique and maintain outside leverage as he defeats the tight end's block. He is responsible for tackling the ballcarrier in the event that the tailback bounces the play outside.

STRONG END: Defender will defeat the offensive tackle's block, and then use the blocker's body to constrict the B gap. It is vital that the end maintains outside leverage in the event that the ballcarrier bounces the play into the C gap.

STRONG TANDEM: As he sees the offensive tackle block the defensive end, the defender must immediately plug the B gap, He will attack the fullback with an inside forearm rip as close to the line of scrimmage as possible and then tackle the ballcarrier.

NOSE: Defender must plug the attackside A gap. As he feels the pressure of the offensive guard (who is attempting *kiss block*), he must force a double-team by getting his hands on the guard and preventing the guard from blocking Mike. As he executes this technique, it is vital that the Nose stays low and does not get driven backwards.

MIKE: If the Nose does his job, Mike should remain unblocked. Mike's landmark is the outside shoulder of the offensive guard's original alignment. Mike will immediately plug this area and tackle the tailback from an inside-out position.

WEAK END: Defender will defeat the offensive tackle's block and chase the play along the heel line. He must look for cutback, counter, and reverse.

WEAK TANDEM: The defender will work downhill, rip through the offensive guard's block and immediately plug the backside A gap.

ROVER: Upon reading flow, defender will begin to retreat to centerfield. When he is sure that the play is a run, he will play the alley.

FREE SAFETY: Since Stud's primary responsibility is containment, the free safety will check the tight end for a delayed pass as he approaches the ballcarrier from an outside-in position.

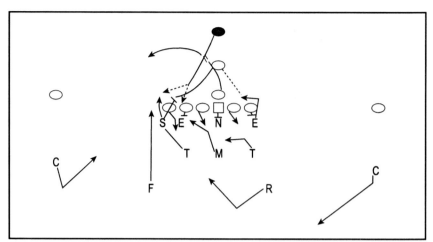

Diagram 3-13

PLAY DESCRIPTION: This play is an I-formation off-tackle play, with the possibility of a quarterback keep.

COACHING POINTS: The keys to stopping this play are the *down-down* call by the Stud, the defensive end forcing a double-team, and the employment of a wrong arm technique by the Stud.

STUD: Stud will give the tandem linebacker a *down-down* call. As he is giving the call, he will close tight to the double-team, close the C gap, and then attack the fullback with an outside forearm rip. By *wrong arming* the fullback, the Stud will spill the play outside.

STRONG END: Defender will first attack the offensive tackle's outside shoulder. As he feels the double-team and hears the *down-down* call, he will immediately force a double-team by getting his hands on the tight end and preventing the tight end from releasing to the next level and blocking the tandem linebacker. It is imperative that end stays low and does not get driven back into the pursuit of the linebackers.

STRONG TANDEM: The backfield action and the *down-down* call will alert the tandem linebacker to scrape outside. He will scrape tight to Stud and be prepared for the ballcarrier to bounce the play outside. Note: if the tandem linebacker sees a C gap window as he is scrapping (because Stud did not close inside), he will immediately close the window.

NOSE: Defender will defeat the center's block, plug the playside A gap, and pursue the ball flat down the line of scrimmage.

MIKE: As reads backfield flow, Mike will immediately work downhill, rip through the offensive guard's' block, secure the B gap, and tackle the ballcarrier from an inside-out position.

WEAK END: Defender will defeat the offensive tackle's block and chase the play along the heel line. He must look for cutback, counter, and reverse. Note: if the quarterback were to fake to the tailback and then bootleg weak side, it is the end's responsibility to contain the quarterback.

WEAK TANDEM: Defender will shuffle two steps parallel to the line, work downhill, rip through the offensive guard's block, check for quarterback bootleg, and then pursue the play from an inside-out position.

ROVER: Defender will first retreat to centerfield. When he is sure that the play is a run, he will provide the defense with alley support.

FREE SAFETY: Defender will check for a tight end delay, and assist in containment. If the quarterback were to keep the ball, it would be the free safety's responsibility to tackle him.

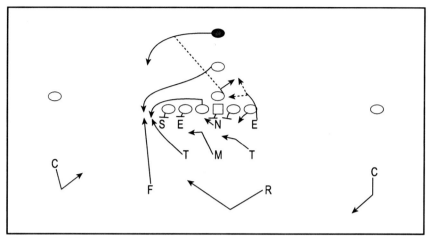

Diagram 3-14

PLAY DESCRIPTION: This play is an I-formation sweep.

COACHING POINTS: The keys to stopping this play are pursuit, penetration, gap closure, and individual techniques versus one-on-one blocks.

STUD: Defender will align in a 9 technique, control the tight end's outside shoulder, maintain outside leverage, keep his shoulders parallel to the line of scrimmage, and force the ballcarrier wide and deep. It is important that Stud rips his inside arm through the tight end's block so that he can get upfield. It is also important that he not get pushed outside in the process.

STRONG END: Defender will control the offensive tackle's outside shoulder, shed the block, and immediately plug the C gap. If possible, he should penetrate the C gap. If not, he will pursue flat down the line and maintain an inside-out position on the ballcarrier.

STRONG TANDEM: As he reads backfield flow and the pull of the offensive guard, the defender will scrape outside. He will rip through the head of the offensive guard with his inside forearm and attempt to blow the play up in the backfield.

NOSE: Defender will jam the center and prevent him from releasing to the next level. He will then plug the playside A gap and pursue the ball flat down the line of scrimmage.

MIKE: Mike will work downhill, plug the B gap, and pursue the ball from an inside-out position. Mike is responsible for cutback.

WEAK END: Defender will first check the quarterback to make certain that he has not faked the toss to the tailback. He will then chase the play along the heel line. He will look for cutback, counter, and reverse.

WEAK TANDEM: Upon reading backfield flow, the defender will shuffle two steps parallel to the line and then work downhill. He will rip through the offensive guard's block (if the guard releases to the second level) and pursue the play from an inside-out position.

ROVER: Upon reading flow, defender will begin to retreat to centerfield. When he is sure that the play is a run, he will play the alley.

FREE SAFETY: Defender will come up quickly and contain the play. He will defeat the fullback's block with an inside forearm rip.

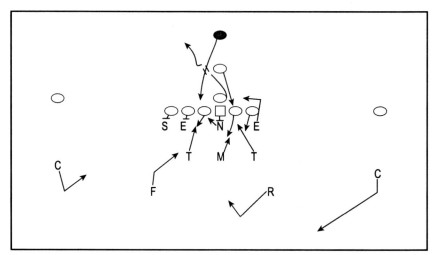

Diagram 3-15

PLAY DESCRIPTION: This play is an I-formation scissors play.

COACHING POINTS: The key to stopping this play is the execution of the two tandems, Mike, and the Nose. Whenever a team runs this type of scheme, instruct Mike to bite on the fullback and the Nose to bite on the tailback (the exception to the Nose's rule would be a head read given to the Nose by the center). Another strategy for stopping the play (when this is one of the offense's bread and butter plays) is to stunt Mike into one A gap and the Nose into the other.

STUD: Defender will align in a 9 technique, control the tight end's outside shoulder, maintain outside leverage, and be prepared for the ballcarrier to bounce the play outside.

STRONG END: Defender will control the offensive tackle's outside shoulder, shed the block and immediately plug the C gap.

STRONG TANDEM: As he reads backfield flow and the offensive tackle's block, the defender will immediately plug the B gap, rip through the offensive guard's block with his inside forearm, and tackle the tailback.

NOSE: If the center drive blocks the Nose and gives the defender no clue as to the play's direction, Mike will stuff and shed the blocker and then plug the A gap in the direction of the tailback's path.

MIKE: This read is a tough one for Mike because the blocking pattern does not help him determine which back is getting the ball; therefore, Mike will tackle the fullback.

WEAK END: The defender will jam the offensive tackle, squeeze the B gap, maintain outside leverage on the fullback, search the fullback for the ball, and then pursue along the heel line.

WEAK TANDEM: The defender will rip through the offensive tackle's block and tackle the fullback.

ROVER: Upon reading flow, defender will begin to retreat to centerfield. When he is sure that the play is a run, he will play the alley.

FREE SAFETY: Defender will maintain outside leverage on the tailback, check the tight end for a delayed pass route, and then approach the ballcarrier from an outside-in position.

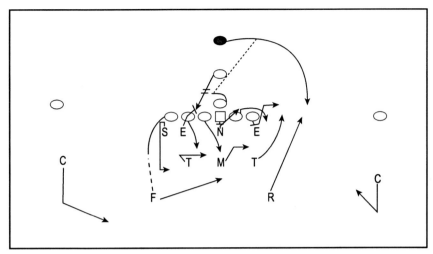

Diagram 3-16

PLAY DESCRIPTION: This play has gained popularity in the NFL in recent years. The quarterback fakes the ball to the fullback, and then turns and flips the ball to the tailback, who goes in the opposite direction.

COACHING POINTS: The read of the pulling guard by Mike, Rover, and the tandem linebacker is an important key that will assist the defense in stopping this play.

STUD: Defender will jam the tight end. As he sees the quarterback flip the ball to the tailback, he will fold back and then pursue the ballcarrier.

STRONG END: Defender will jam the offensive tackle and tackle the fullback as deep in the backfield as possible.

STRONG TANDEM: As he sees the offensive tackle block inside, the defender will begin scrapping to the C gap, but as he sees the quarterback flip the ball to the tailback, he will immediately *put on the brakes*, reverse direction, and pursue the ball from an inside-out position.

NOSE: Defender will attack, stuff, and shed the center's block. Because he is reading the center-guard triangle, he will see the pulling guard. Upon seeing this, he will immediately plug the playside A gap and pursue the ballcarrier flat down the line.

MIKE: Mike's keys will also enable him to see the pulling guard. As he makes this read, he will immediately plug the playside B gap and pursue the play from an inside-out position.

WEAK END: Defender must defeat the offensive tackle's block and gain penetration by ripping his inside arm through the tackle's block. He will then pursue the ball from an inside-out position.

WEAK TANDEM: Upon reading the pulling guard the defender will scrape outside and assist in containment. If blocked by the pulling guard, he will rip through the guard's block with his inside forearm.

ROVER: As he reads the pulling guard and the action of the tailback, the defender will come up and contain the play.

FREE SAFETY: As he sees the quarterback flip the ball to the tailback, the defender will first check the tight end for a throwback pass. When he is sure that the play is a run, he will purse the ballcarrier.

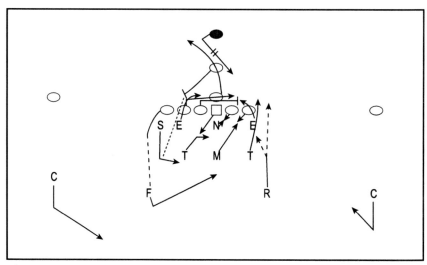

Diagram 3-17

PLAY DESCRIPTION: This play is the ever-popular weak side counter trey.

COACHING POINTS: If the weakside end is able to close tough to the inside and cut block the pulling guard—thus preventing the tackle from leading through the hole, then this play has little chance of success.

STUD: Defender will jam the tight end. As he sees the action of the tailback and quarterback, he will check the fullback for the counter-trey pass (naked boot). When he is absolutely certain that the play is a run, he will fold back and pursue the ballcarrier.

STRONG END: Defender will first take on the block of the fullback. When he is certain that the fullback's intent is to block and not run a pass route, the end will chase the play along the heel line. Note: the end is responsible for quarterback containment versus the counter-trey (naked boot) pass.

STRONG TANDEM: As he sees the guard and tackle pull, the defender will work downhill, plug the backside A gap, rip through the center's block, and pursue the play from an inside-out position.

NOSE: As the center blocks away, the defender will immediately step to and plug his opposite A gap. He must hold his ground and spill the play outside.

MIKE: As Mike sees the guard and tackle pull, he will immediately plug the playside B gap. Mike must attack the guard's block as close to the line as possible and spill the play outside.

WEAK END: Defender must jam the tackle and simultaneously close to the inside. His job is to nullify the pulling linemen by cut blocking the pulling guard.

WEAK TANDEM: Defender will scrape tight to the defensive end and tackle the ballcarrier as he tries to bounce the play outside.

ROVER: As he reads the backfield action and the blocking scheme, the defender will come up quickly and contain the play.

FREE SAFETY: Defender will first check the tight end for the counter-trey pass. When he is sure that the play is a run, he will pursue the ballcarrier.

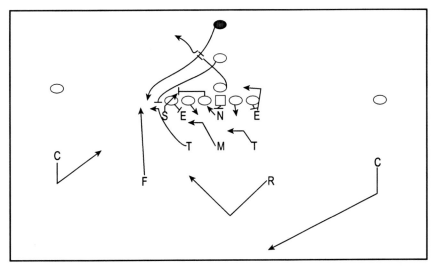

Diagram 3-18

PLAY DESCRIPTION: This play is an off-tackle, I-formation slant play with the fullback leading.

COACHING POINTS: Defenders plugging their gaps and forcing the ballcarrier to bounce the play outside is the key to stopping this play.

STUD: Defender will jam tight end, give the strong end a *down-down* call, and simultaneously close the C gap. He will then attack the pulling guard with his outside forearm (wrong arm) and spill the play outside.

STRONG END: Defender will jam the tackle, and upon hearing the *down-down* call, he will fight outside pressure, hold his ground, and not get driven back.

STRONG TANDEM: As he reads his keys, he will scrape tight to the Stud, attack the fullback with his inside forearm, maintain outside leverage, and tackle the tailback as he bounces the play outside.

NOSE: Defender will see the guard pull as he stuffs and separates from the center's block. He will then plug the playside A gap and pursue the ball from an inside-out position.

MIKE: Defender will work downhill and plug the B gap by attacking the tackle's block with an inside forearm rip. Mike is responsible for cutback; it is therefore imperative that he maintains an inside-out relationship with the ballcarrier.

WEAK END: Defender will destroy the tackle's block and chase the play along the heel line. He must look for cutback, counter, and reverse.

WEAK TANDEM: Upon reading backfield flow, the defender will shuffle two steps parallel to the line and then work downhill. He will then will rip through the offensive guard's block and pursue the play from an inside-out position.

ROVER: Upon reading flow, defender will begin to retreat to centerfield. When he is sure that the play is a run, he will play the alley.

FREE SAFETY: Defender will quickly move toward the line of scrimmage as he checks for a tight end delay. When he is certain that the play is a run, he will assist in containment.

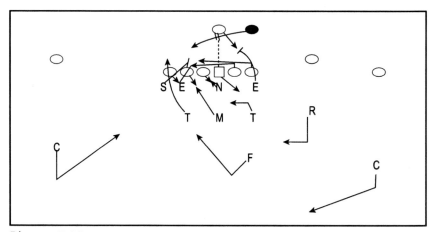

Diagram 3-19

PLAY DESCRIPTION: This play is one of the most popular in football today: the strongside counter-trey read. This play is an option; the quarterback will either give the ball to the running back or keep it—depending upon the action of the weakside defensive end. If the end chases the play, the quarterback will keep the ball; if he does not, the quarterback will give the ball to the running back.

COACHING POINTS: The keys to stopping this play are the techniques employed by the strong and weak ends.

STUD: As he reads the tight end's block, Stud must close the C gap. He will not give the strong end a down-down block because this would alert the defensive end to fight outside pressure. Instead, the defensive end should close tough inside and nullify the blocks of the pulling linemen. After closing the C gap, Stud will maintain outside leverage on the running back and anticipate that the play will spill outside.

STRONG END: Defender must jam the tackle and simultaneously close to the inside. His job is to nullify the pulling linemen by cut blocking the pulling guard.

STRONG TANDEM: Defender will scrape tight to the Stud and tackle the ballcarrier as he tries to bounce the play outside.

NOSE: As the center blocks away, the defender will immediately step to and plug his opposite A gap. He must hold his ground and spill the play outside.

MIKE: As Mike sees the guard and tackle pull, he will immediately plug the playside B gap. Mike must attack the guard's block as close to the line as possible and spill the play outside.

WEAK END: As he sees the tackle pull, the defender will immediately tackle the quarterback.

WEAK TANDEM: As he sees the guard and tackle pull, the defender will first check the quarterback to make certain that the defensive end has tackled him. He will then work downhill, plug the A gap, rip through the center's block, and pursue the play from an inside-out position.

ROVER: Defender is involved in coverage.

FREE SAFETY: Defender will provide the defense with alley support.

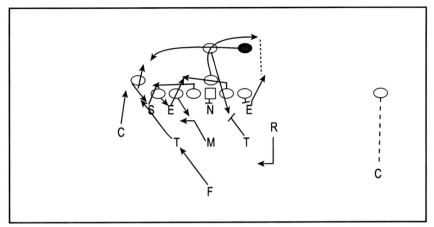

Diagram 3-20

PLAY DESCRIPTION: This play is a wing-T buck sweep.

COACHING POINTS: Like the option, the wing-T forces specific defenders to play assignment football. Every defender must therefore check his assignment before flying to the ball. Also versus the wing-T, defenders should not give down-down calls because the defenders need to jam down blocks, gain penetration, and knock pulling linemen of their intended tracts.

STUD: Defender will jam tight end and immediately close the C gap. He will ignore the down block of the wingback. Instead, he will attempt to gain penetration, *wrong arm* the pulling guard, and spill the play outside.

STRONG END: Defender will jam the tackle and immediately close the B gap. He will ignore the down block of the tight end, attempt to gain penetration, and either blow the play up in the backfield, or knock the back side guard off his tract.

STRONG TANDEM: As he reads his keys, he will scrape tight to the Stud, attack the wingback (who will be working to the second level) with his inside forearm, maintain outside leverage, and tackle the halfback as he bounces the play outside.

NOSE: Defender will see the guards pull as he stuffs and separates from the center's block. He will then plug the playside A gap and pursue the ball from an inside-out position.

MIKE: Defender will work downhill and plug the B gap by attacking the tackle's block with an inside forearm rip. Mike is responsible for cutback; it is therefore imperative that he maintains an inside-out relationship with the ballcarrier.

WEAK END: Defender will destroy the tackle's block and then check the quarterback for the bootleg (run or pass).

WEAK TANDEM: Defender will immediately attack the line of scrimmage and tackle the fullback.

ROVER: Defender will first check the quarterback for bootleg. Next, he will check the wingback for counter. He will then pursue the ball.

FREE SAFETY: Defender will first check the wingback for counter or pass. When he is certain that the play is the buck sweep, he will fill the alley.

CORNERBACK: Defender will quickly move toward the line of scrimmage and contain the play.

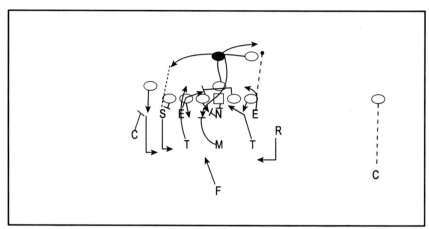

Diagram 3-21

PLAY DESCRIPTION: This play is a wing-T trap.

COACHING POINTS: The number of defenders aligned between the offensive tackles gives the defense a mathematical advantage in stopping this play.

STUD: The defender will attack the tight end, defeat his block and create separation. Before folding back inside, Stud will check the halfback for a screen.

STRONG END: The defender will jam the tackle and immediately close the B gap. He will attack the trapper with an outside forearm rip and spill the play outside.

STRONG TANDEM: As he sees the offensive tackle release inside, the defender will scrape tight to the tail of the defensive end. If he were blocked by the tight end (not illustrated) the strong tandem would defeat the tight end's block with an outside forearm rip and hang tough in the B gap.

NOSE: The defender will plug the playside A gap as he sees the guard pull. When he feels pressure from the play side guard (who is attempting a *kiss block*), the defender will get his hands on the guard and force a double-team. It is vital that the Nose holds his ground, creates a pile, and does not get driven back.

MIKE: The defender will scrape to the B gap and tackle the fullback.

WEAK END: The defender will jam the offensive tackle, check the quarterback for a keep, and then chase the play along the heel line.

WEAK TANDEM: The defender will work downhill, rip through the offensive tackle's block with his outside forearm, and plug the backside A gap.

ROVER: Defender will first check the quarterback for bootleg. Next, he will check the wingback for counter, and then pursue the ball.

FREE SAFETY: Defender will first check the wingback for counter or pass. When he is certain that the play is a run, he will fill the alley.

CORNERBACK: Defender will jam the wingback and then fold back inside when he is sure that the play is a run.

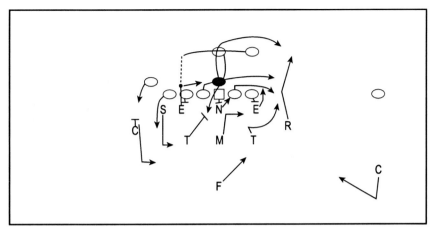

Diagram 3-22

PLAY DESCRIPTION: This play is a wing-T quarterback bootleg run.

COACHING POINTS: Defenders reading and reacting to the pulling guards are the keys to stopping this play.

STUD: The defender will read backfield flow and the tight end's release. He will then sink and check the tight end for a bootleg pass pattern before pursuing the ball.

STRONG END: The defender will defeat the tackle's block and then check the halfback for a screen pattern before chasing the ball.

STRONG TANDEM: As he sees the offensive guard pull, the defender will work downhill and plug the backside A gap. Since the fullback is faking a run into this gap, the linebacker will make certain that the fullback does not have the ball before pursuing the play. If in doubt, he will tackle the fullback.

NOSE: The defender will plug the playside A gap as he sees the guards pull. He will then pursue the play flat down the line of scrimmage.

MIKE: As he sees the guards pull, the defender work downhill and plug the playside B gap. If he sees a window as he is plugging the B gap, he will penetrate the line of scrimmage and tackle the quarterback in the backfield. If no window exists, Mike will pursue the ball from an inside-out position.

WEAK END: The defender will defeat the offensive tackle's block and then work outside and assist in containing the quarterback.

WEAK TANDEM: As he sees the guard pull, the defender will scrape outside and assist in containing the quarterback.

ROVER: As he reads backfield action and the pulling guard, the defender will quickly penetrate the line of scrimmage and contain the quarterback.

FREE SAFETY: Defender will first check the wingback for counter or pass. When he is certain that the play is a run, he will fill the alley.

CORNERBACK: The defender will read backfield flow and the wingback's release. He will then sink and check the wingback for a bootleg pass pattern before pursuing the ball.

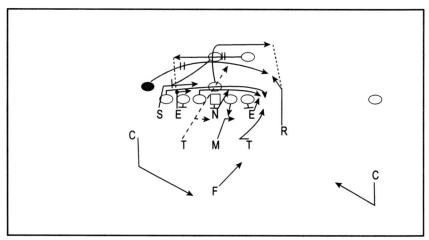

Diagram 3-23

PLAY DESCRIPTION: This play is a wingback counter.

COACHING POINTS: Defenders reading and reacting to pulling linemen, and the cornerback's counter alert are the key to stopping this play.

STUD: As the defender sees both the tight end and wingback pull, the defender will defeat the fullback's block, check the halfback for the ball, and then chase the play along the heel line.

STRONG END: The defender will defeat the tackle's block and then check the halfback for a screen pattern before chasing the ball.

STRONG TANDEM: As he sees the guard pull, the defender will work downhill and plug the backside A gap. If he sees a window that will enable him to blow up the play in the backfield, he will penetrate it and tackle the wingback for a loss; if no window exists, he will pursue the ball from an inside-out position.

NOSE: The defender will plug the playside A gap as he sees the guard pull. He will then pursue the play flat down the line of scrimmage.

MIKE: As he sees the guard pull, the defender work downhill, rip through the offensive guard's block, secure the playside B gap, and then pursue the play from an inside-out position.

WEAK END: The defender will defeat the tackle's block by gaining separation and ripping his inside arm past the tackle's outstretched arms. He will then penetrate the line of scrimmage.

WEAK TANDEM: The defender will begin shuffling inside, As he hears the cornerback scream counter he will reverse direction, scrape outside, and assist in containment.

ROVER: As the defender hears the cornerback scream *counter* the defender will quickly penetrate the line of scrimmage and contain the play.

FREE SAFETY: Defender will first check the wingback for counter. When he sees and hears that a *counter* is in progress, he will fill the alley.

CORNERBACK: Defender will scream *counter*, fold back, and then take the correct angle of pursuit.

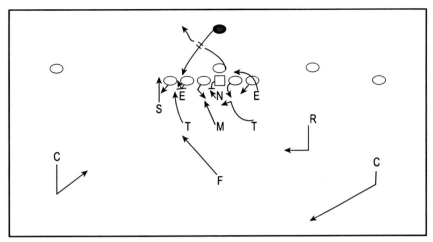

Diagram 3-24

PLAY DESCRIPTION: This play is an aceback inside zone play.

COACHING POINTS: The two keys to stopping this play are first, playside defenders controlling their assigned gaps, and second, backside defenders pursuing the ball from an inside-out position and denying the running back a cutback lane.

STUD: The defender will approach the line of scrimmage quickly, attack the tight end's block, maintain outside leverage, contain the running back, and force him to cut back into pursuit.

STRONG END: Defender will control the offensive tackle's outside shoulder, shed the block, and immediately plug the C gap. If possible, he should penetrate the C gap; if not, he will hold his ground and attack the ballcarrier from an inside-out position.

STRONG TANDEM: The defender should remain unblocked. He should therefore mirror the path of the ballcarrier and make that tackle at the line of scrimmage.

NOSE: This player has the most important job on the entire defense. He must jam the center and prevent the center from releasing to the next level. If he is not capable of doing this, the entire defense will quickly fall apart. As he is jamming the center, his momentum will automatically enable him to plug the playside A gap.

MIKE: Mike will work downhill, rip through the offensive guards block, and plug the B gap. It is important that Mike remains close to the line of scrimmage and does not open up any alleys for the ballcarrier.

WEAK END: The defender will then chase the play along the heel line. He will look for cutback, counter, and reverse. Because he is unblocked, he has an excellent chance of tackling the ballcarrier from behind (especially if the ballcarrier hesitates or cuts back).

WEAK TANDEM: Upon reading backfield flow, the defender will shuffle two steps parallel to the line and then work downhill. He will rip through the offensive guard's block and pursue the play from an inside-out position.

ROVER: Defender is involved in coverage and will pursue the ball only when he is absolutely certain that the play is a run.

FREE SAFETY: Defender will provide the defense with alley support.

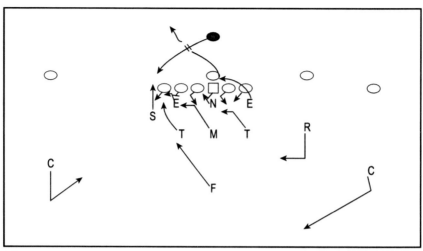

Diagram 3-25

PLAY DESCRIPTION: This play is an aceback stretch play.

COACHING POINTS: The keys to stopping this play are almost identical to stopping the inside zone. The primary responsibility for successfully defending this play rests upon the Stud because he is responsible for containment.

STUD: The defender will immediately attack the line of scrimmage, rip through the tight end's block with an inside forearm, and force the ballcarrier to either cutback, or redirect his tact wide and deep.

STRONG END: Defender will control the offensive tackle's outside shoulder, shed the block, and immediately plug the C gap. If possible, he should penetrate the C gap; if not, he will pursue flat down the line of scrimmage.

STRONG TANDEM: The defender will scrape outside and secure the C gap.

NOSE: The defender must jam the center and prevent the center from releasing to the next level. As he is jamming the center, his momentum will automatically enable him to plug the playside A gap. He will then pursue the ball flat down the line of scrimmage.

MIKE: Mike will work downhill, rip through the offensive guard's block, and plug the B gap. He will then pursue the ball from an inside-out position.

WEAK END: The defender will then chase the play along the heel line. He will look for cutback, counter, and reverse.

WEAK TANDEM: Upon reading backfield flow, the defender will shuffle two steps parallel to the line and then work downhill. He will rip through the offensive guard's block and pursue the play from an inside-out position.

ROVER: Defender is involved in coverage and will pursue the ball only when he is absolutely certain that the play is a run.

FREE SAFETY: Defender will provide the defense with alley support.

4

Man-to-Man Techniques for Defensive Backs

The purpose of this chapter is to explain in detail the man-to-man techniques used by defensive backs in the 3-3-5. As mentioned in Chapter 1, the three defensive backs are referred to as the field corner, boundary corner, and free safety. The field corner is the best cover corner; he usually covers the #1 receiver aligned toward the wide side of the field (exception: some game plans may require him to cover an opponent's best receiver). The boundary corner covers the #1 receiver aligned into the boundary. When any variation of cover 1 is employed, the boundary corner will use an outside bump technique because he will receive inside help from the free safety. When the ball is in the middle of the field, or when any variation of zero coverage is used, the boundary corner will employ the same techniques as the field corner.

Field Corner Techniques

Stance, Alignment, and Responsibility

The defender will assume a stance and alignment that will enable him to use his peripheral vision to see both the quarterback and the receiver. The defender will:

- Concentrate on covering #1 and not concern himself with run support unless he is absolutely certain that the ball has crossed the line of scrimmage.
- Align himself one yard inside of #1 and seven to eight yards deep.
- Keep his outside foot up (toe to heel relationship) with his weight on his front foot.
- Keep a narrow base with his feet close together.
- Let his arms hang loosely.
- Drop his hips and round his back slightly so that his nose is in front of his toes.

Backpedal Technique

Before the snap, the defender will anticipate potential routes based upon the receiver's split. If a receiver has a wide split, the defender will anticipate an inside route; if the receiver's alignment is tight, the defender should expect an outside route. When backpedaling, the defender will:

- Maintain inside leverage on #1 and never allow the receiver to get head up with himself.
- Keep a good forward lean as he backpedals.
- Take an initial three-step read. The defender will control the speed of his backpedal during his first three steps to determine the depth of the quarterback's drop, which will enable him to react quickly to patterns in which the quarterback takes three steps (hitch, out, slant, etc.). Although the defender's primary focus is the quarterback during his three-step read, he must also be able to see the receiver out of his periphery.
- Push off his front foot when the ball is snapped, and make the first step with the back foot.
- Keep his weight on the balls of the feet.
- Keep feet close to the ground and take small to medium steps. It is a serious mistake to over-stride.
- Keep his arms relaxed and bent at a 90-degree angle, with his arms pumping vigorously when he begins his backpedal.

- Maintain a cushion of approximately three to four yards from the receiver.
- Keep his shoulders parallel to the line, and not turn them unless his cushion is broken.
- Turn his hips to the receiver.
- Mirror the receiver's movements and keep his outside shoulder on the receiver's inside shoulder.
- Control the speed of his backpedal. When the receiver makes his break, the defender must be under control and able to gather and break quickly in the direction of the receivers break.
- Concentrate on the base of the receiver's numbers until the receiver makes his final break. He must not look at the receiver's head.
- Anticipate the receiver's break. Looks for the receiver to changes his forward lean, begins to chop his feet, or widen his base.
- Turn and run with the receiver, keeping his body between the ball and the receiver whenever the receiver gets within two yards.

Plant and Drive

When the receiver makes his final break, the defender will:

- Drop his shoulder in the direction of the receiver's break, and explode in that direction.
- Quickly close the cushion between himself and the receiver, and break parallel to the receiver's break.
- Maintain concentration on the receiver.
- Not look for the ball until he has closed his cushion and he sees the receiver look for the ball.

Playing the Ball

When the ball is thrown, the defender should:

- Attack the ball at its highest point when attempting an interception.
- Play the ball—not the receiver—when the ball is inside of the defender and the receiver is outside of him.
- Play the ball through the receiver's upfield shoulder when the receiver is between the defender and the ball.
- Never cut in front of the receiver to make an interception unless he is absolutely sure that he can get two hands on the ball.

- Try to catch the ball or break up a pass with two hands, not one.
- Knock the ball toward the ground, never up in the air.
- Try to strip the ball out of the receiver's hands if the receiver catches it.
- Yell "Oski" and head toward the nearest sideline whenever he makes an interception.

Boundary Corner Outside Bump Technique

Stance, Alignment, and Responsibility

When the ball is on the hash and cover 1 is being employed, the boundary corner will:

- Line up with his nose on the outside shoulder of # 1.
- Keep his outside foot up and tilt his butt slightly toward the sideline.
- Line up two yards deep, but this may vary from an alignment that crowds the line of scrimmage to one that is five yards deep.
- Position his hands at the midsection in a ready position to jam the receiver.
- Focus his eyes on the midsection of the receiver.
- Jam #1's inside releases, and force the receiver into the free safety.
- Shuffle his feet parallel to the line of scrimmage as he jams #1.
- Deny #1 an outside release.
- Push #1 as far inside as he can, and not allow any separation after the initial bump.

Inside Bump Man Techniques for Cornerbacks

The advantages of an inside bump technique is that it limits the offense's pass route selection and disrupts the timing between the quarterback and the receivers. It also gives the pass rushers additional time to get to the quarterback. Any time a coach feels that a corner can adequately cover his designated receiver with an inside bump technique, he may consider its use. When employing this technique, the defender will:

- Line up on the inside eye of #1. Normal depth is crowding the line of scrimmage to one to two yards deep.
- Keep his feet shoulder width apart and parallel.
- Keep his eyes focused on the receiver's midsection.
- Collision all inside releases with his inside arm (the arm closest to the quarterback). The defender should punch the receiver in the sternum with his palm out. He must be careful not to overextend when punching the receiver.

- Not move until the receiver moves. When the receiver releases, the defender will shuffle in the direction of the receiver's release, and not over-stride while shuffling. The defender will punch while shuffling, and be careful not to open his hips until the route has been established.

- Not be faked or juked by the receiver. He must be aware that if the receiver makes a hard outside move, he is likely going to come back and run an inside route. If on the other hand, the receiver makes a hard inside move, he is likely going to run an outside route.

- Concentrate on the receiver and stay within a yard of him as he covers his route. The defender must not peek back at the quarterback; he will find the ball when the receiver looks for it.

- Use a speed turn to get back into position if the receiver gets the defender to open his hips and is able to get underneath the defender. After the speed turn, the defender will attempt to cut off the receiver's route and sprint to the cut-off point.

The Free Safety's Cover 1 Technique

Stance, Alignment, and Technique

When cover 1 is employed, the free safety will:

- Line up 8-15 yards deep (depending upon down and distance and offensive tendency).
- Line up directly in front of the center when the ball is in the middle of the field.
- Line up on the outside shoulder of the offensive tackle (toward the wide side of the field) when the ball is on the hash or when the offense splits two or more receivers toward one side of the field.
- Assume a parallel stance (a slight stagger is permissible if the defender feels more comfortable in this position).
- Put his weight on the balls of his feet with his heels slightly raised off the ground.
- Bend his knees slightly and lower his hips.
- Bend his waist slightly, which will cause his back to appear slightly rounded.
- Relax his hands and arms and allow them to hang loosely.
- Key the ball through an uncovered lineman.

Techniques and Responsibilities Versus the Pass

The defender's first three steps are extremely important because they will enable him to read the play and to begin moving toward the best possible position to make a great play. He must keep his eyes on all of the receivers being funneled inside because it is his responsibility to provide deep help in covering these receivers. As he reads pass, the free safety will:

- Sprint to a position that will place him between the receivers who are being funneled into him. Versus a two-back pro formation, those receivers will be the tight end and X.
- Continue to gain depth by back pedaling or sprinting until the quarterback has finished setting up.
- Stay deeper than any of the receivers who are being funneled into him.
- Follow the same basic guidelines as the field corner when reacting to a pass.

Techniques and Responsibilities Versus the Run

The free safety is responsible for providing alley support to all running plays. When providing alley support, the defender will:

- Go directly to the ball between the primary force player and the defensive end.
- Approach the ballcarrier from an inside-out position and expect that the ballcarrier will cut back.
- Protect his legs and prevent blockers from getting into his body. The defender should try to avoid the blocker if at all possible (without taking himself out of the play). When avoiding the blocker becomes impossible, the defender should become the hammer—not the nail—and punish the blocker.
- React to crack blocks. The defender whose receiver is cracking will give the free safety a crack-crack call. The free safety will then attack and/or cover the cracking receiver and the other defender will replace the free safety and support the run.

5

Covering Individual Pass Routes

The purpose of this chapter is to analyze for the specific loose man-to-man techniques that will be used by defensive backs to cover the basic routes of the passing game.

Slant Route

The receiver will most likely break inside at a 45-degree angle on his third or fourth step. He may try to stem the defender outside on his release. The quarterback should throw the ball as the receiver makes his break. The defender must maintain inside leverage and keep his shoulders parallel to the line of scrimmage as he back pedals. He must use his peripheral vision to not only see the receiver but to also recognize the quarterback's drop. The defender's three-step read will alert him that a quick pass is in progress (the quarterback's shortened second step and/or low front shoulder are the defender's key indicators). Once the slant is recognized, the defender should plant and drive to the interception point, which is a point approximately four to six yards in front of the receiver. Some contact may result as the ball is thrown. If the receiver catches the ball, the defender must ensure the tackle and rip the ball out of the receiver's possession.

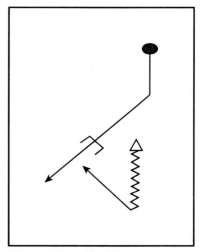

Diagram 5-1: Slant Route

5-6 Yard Out Route

The quarterback should throw the ball as the receiver makes his break. The defender's three-step read will alert him that a quick pass is in progress. Once the out route is recognized, the defender will plant, drive, and break to the receiver's upfield shoulder. The defender must ensure the tackle with his right arm over the right shoulder pad of the receiver and rip the arm or punch the ball with his left hand. A defender should never undercut the ball unless he has read the route and is in perfect position.

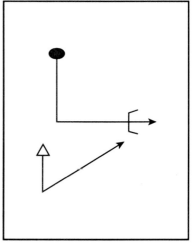

Diagram 5-2: 5-6 Yard Out Route

5-6 Hitch Route

The quarterback should throw the ball as the receiver makes his break. The defender's three-step read will alert him that a quick pass is in progress. Once the hitch is recognized, the defender should plant and drive to the upfield shoulder of the receiver. The defender must ensure the tackle with his right arm over the right shoulder pad of the receiver and rip the arm or punch the ball with the left hand.

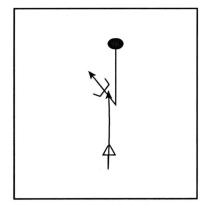

Diagram 5-3: 5-6 Hitch Route

Hitch and Go Route

Once the hitch is recognized, the defender should plant and drive to the outside shoulder of the receiver. When the quarterback pumps the ball, the receiver will turn and run the go. If the defender is in good position, he will collision the receiver as he runs his go. The route should be eliminated at this point. If the receiver gets by the defender, he must run with him, trying to cut off the route. See how to play the fade for more info.

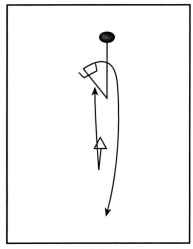

Diagram 5-4: Hitch and Go Route

Curl Route

The defender must maintain inside leverage and keep his shoulders parallel to the line of scrimmage as he back pedals. The defender should be able to sense the receiver's break by the quarterback's drop. The receiver will break his pattern at about 12 yards if the quarterback takes a five-step drop and at about 16 yards if the quarterback takes a seven-step drop. When the receiver begins to chop his feet or raises his pad level, the defender should begin to plant his feet. As the receiver breaks his route toward the quarterback, the defender will drive to the interception point. He will ensure the tackle with his right arm over the right shoulder pad, and rip or punch with the left hand.

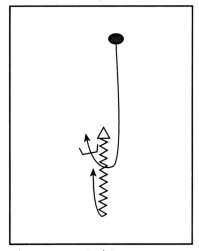

Diagram 5-5: Curl Route

In Route

The defender must maintain inside leverage and keep his shoulders parallel to the line of scrimmage as he back pedals. The defender should be able to sense the receiver's break by the quarterback's drop. The receiver will break his pattern at about 12 yards if the quarterback takes a five-step drop, and about 16 yards if the quarterback takes a seven-step drop. When the receiver breaks to the in and begins running down the line, the defender must plant and drive to the upfield shoulder of the receiver. More than likely the defender will be right behind the receiver. When the ball is thrown, the defender will ensure the tackle with his right arm and rip or punch with his left arm to try to get the ball out.

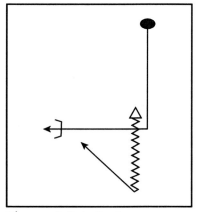

Diagram 5-6: In Route

Post Route

The defender must maintain inside leverage and keep his shoulders parallel to the line of scrimmage as he back pedals. The defender should be able to sense the receiver's break by the quarterback's drop. When the receiver breaks to the post, the defender must turn his hips to the inside and drive to a point in front of the receiver, allowing no more than one yard separation. The defender will be right behind the receiver, on his hip pocket. When the ball is thrown, the defender will rip with the right arm and strip with the left hand.

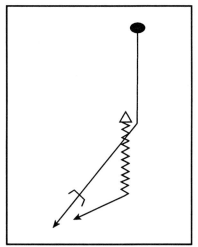

Diagram 5-7: Post Route

Post-Corner Route

Initially, the defender will use the same rules as covering the post pattern. When the receiver breaks to the corner, the defender will use a speed turn to tract the receiver's break. When employing the speed turn, the defender must plant with his inside foot, whip his head around, and drive hard to the corner.

Diagram 5-8: Post-Corner Route

Fade Route

The defender's three-step read will alert him that a quick pass is in progress. The defender should be able to recognize the fade route immediately. The defender must keep a three-yard cushion between himself and the receiver. If the cushion is broken, the defender must turn his hips to the receiver and begin to run to cut off the fade route—achieved by leaning the outside shoulder pad into the receiver. The defender must never look back at the quarterback. As the ball nears the receiver, the defender will rip up through the receiver's arms and strip the ball out of the receiver's hands.

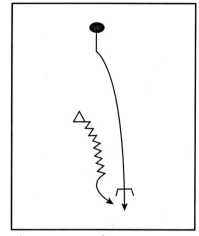

Diagram 5-9: Fade Route

Comeback Route

The defender must maintain inside leverage and keep his shoulders parallel to the line of scrimmage as he back pedals. The defender will rule out a fade pattern because of the quarterback's drop. After the receiver goes 12 yards, the defender will expect a break at about 16 yards. When the receiver makes his break, the defender must plant his inside leg and drive to the receiver's upfield shoulder. The defender will probably get there as the ball is thrown. The defender will ensure the tackle with the left arm, and rip or punch the ball with his right hand.

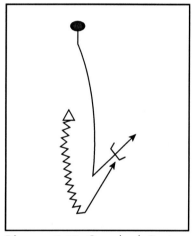

Diagram 5-10: Comeback Route

Dig Route

The dig route is one of the most difficult patterns in football to cover. Initially, the defender will use the same rules for covering the post. As the receiver begins his second break parallel to the line of scrimmage, the defender must plant with his outside leg and drive to the receiver. The defender will be trailing the receiver but must be in a position to make the tackle or break up the pass.

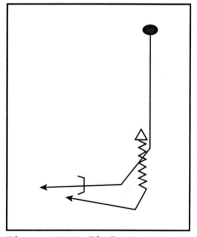

Diagram 5-11: Dig Route

Flag Route

Initially, this route is covered just like a post route. When the receiver breaks to the corner, the defender must turn his hips to the outside and drive to a point in front of the receiver. Allow no more than one yard of separation. The defender will be on the receiver's hip pocket. When the ball is thrown, the defender will rip with the right arm and strip with the left hand.

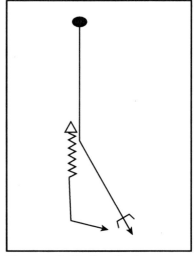

Diagram 5-12: Flag Route

6

Basic Stunts and Principles of Stunting

Stunt Terminology

The purpose of this chapter is to lay the foundation for a relatively simple, but extremely comprehensive stunt package that easily adapts itself to multiple pass coverages—and employs a minimum of verbiage. When introducing the basic terminology used to denote essential defensive stunt concepts, keep in mind that these terms will often be added to other terms to create a complete stunt. At first glance these concepts may seem extremely complex and burdensome, but in reality they are extremely simple. Having used them for over twenty years, a player has yet to complain that they were too hard to master. The great thing about these terms is that they enable a defensive coach to subject an offense to almost any type manipulative stunt tactic that he is capable of envisioning.

M (Diagram 6-1): This stunt involves two players, Mike and Nose. These two players will stunt into the two A gaps. Mike will either tap or tell Nose which gap he should slant into, and Mike will blitz into the opposite gap.

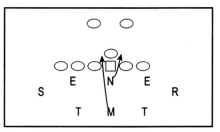
Diagram 6-1

S (Diagram 6-2): This stunt involves the strong end and strong tandem. The strong tandem will direct the strong end's charge. If the strong end is directed to slant inside, he will attack the guard's near shoulder, and the strong tandem will stunt through the outside shoulder of the offensive tackle. If not directed inside, the strong end will employ his basic 5 technique, and the strong tandem will blitz through the outside shoulder of the offensive guard.

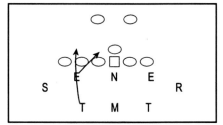
Diagram 6-2

W (Diagram 6-3): This stunt is identical to S, with the exception that it involves the weak tandem and weak end.

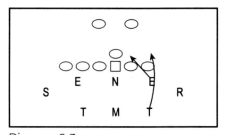
Diagram 6-3

Snake (Diagram 6-4): This stunt is a delayed reaction to pass. Versus run, Stud will employ his normal 8 technique, but when confronted by a pass, he will delay blitz through the strongside B gap. This stunt will be used in conjunction with another strongside stunt (such as S), in which some other defender has already penetrated the strongside B gap. Blitzing two defenders through the same gap is commonly referred to as a *twin stunt*.

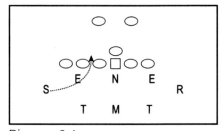
Diagram 6-4

Rat (Diagram 6-5): This stunt is the weakside version of snake.

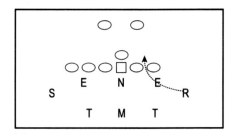
Diagram 6-5

Sting (Diagram 6-6): This stunt is another *delayed twin stunt*. The strong tandem will employ his normal base read technique versus run. However, when confronted by a pass he will delay blitz through the weakside A gap.

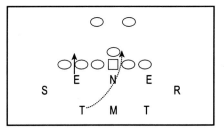

Diagram 6-6

Wing (Diagram 6-7): This stunt is the weakside version of sting.

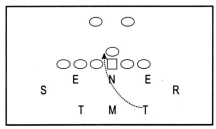

Diagram 6-7

Nose (Diagram 6-8): This stunt is a delayed reaction to a pass by the Nose. It is also a *twin stunt*. Nose will employ his 0 technique versus run. Versus pass, he will delay twist through the strongside B gap.

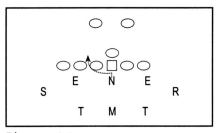

Diagram 6-8

New (Diagram 6-9): This stunt is the weakside version of Nose.

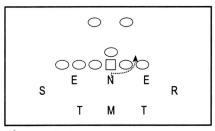

Diagram 6-9

Tap (Diagram 6-10): This stunt is a combination of both S and W.

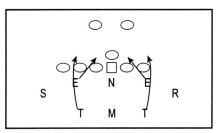

Diagram 6-10

Triple Tap (Diagram 6-11): This stunt is a combination of M, S, and W.

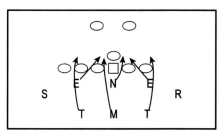

Diagram 6-11

Spy S (Diagram 6-12): When this stunt is used, the strong end will always play his 5 technique and secure the C gap versus run. Versus pass, he will pretend to rush the quarterback; however, instead of rushing the quarterback, the strong end will cover the near back man-to-man if the near back should release for a pass pattern. Because the strong end will always play his 5 technique, the strong tandem will always blitz through the outside shoulder of the offensive guard when this term is used. This term also directs the Stud to rush from the edge, contain the quarterback and strongside run, and chase weakside run.

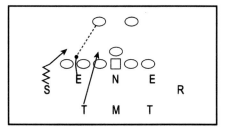

Diagram 6-12

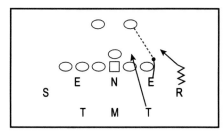

Diagram 6-13

Spy W (Diagram 6-13): This stunt is identical to spy S, with the exception that this is a weakside stunt.

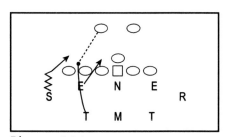

Diagram 6-14

Bronco S (Diagram 6-14): This stunt is identical to spy S with the exception that that the term Bronco directs the strong end and strong tandem to switch assignments.

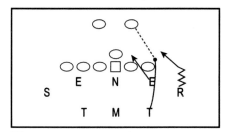

Diagram 6-15

Bronco W (Diagram 6-15): This stunt is the weakside version of Bronco S.

Spy Tap (Diagram 6-16): This stunt is a combination of two previously mentioned stunts, spy S and spy W. It gives the offense the illusion that seven defenders are rushing the quarterback.

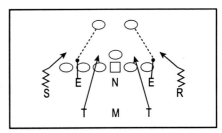

Diagram 6-16

Bronco Tap (Diagram 6-17): This blend of Bronco S and Bronco W also gives the offense the illusion that seven defenders are rushing the quarterback.

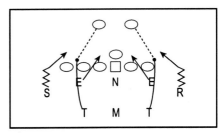

Diagram 6-17

Spy Triple Tap (Diagram 6-18): This stunt adds M to spy tap, and gives the offense the illusion that eight defenders are rushing the quarterback.

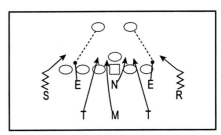

Diagram 6-18

Bronco Triple Tap (Diagram 6-19): This stunt adds M to Bronco tap.

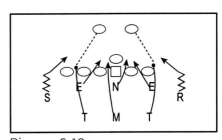

Diagram 6-19

Sam (Diagram 6-20): This stunt is a combination of S and M.

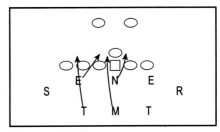

Diagram 6-20

Sax (Diagram 6-21):   When this stunt is employed, the strong end will play his normal 5 technique, the strong tandem will blitz through the strong A gap, Mike will blitz through the strong B gap, and the Nose will slant into the weak A gap.

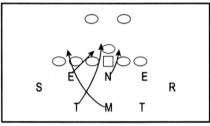

Diagram 6-21

Shark (Diagram 6-22): This stunt directs the strong end to slant into the B gap, the Nose to slant into the weak A gap, the strong tandem to blitz through the strong A gap, and Mike to blitz through the strong B gap.

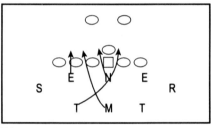

Diagram 6-22

Sex (Diagram 6-23): This stunt has the strong end playing his normal 5 technique, the Nose slanting into the strong A gap, Mike blitzing through the strong B gap, and the strong tandem blitzing through the weak A gap. Like sax and shark, sex burdens the offensive line by forcing it to block a maze of crossing defenders.

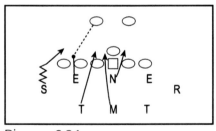

Diagram 6-23

Spy Sam (Diagram 6-24): This stunt adds spy to Sam and gives the offense the illusion of a four-man strongside rush.

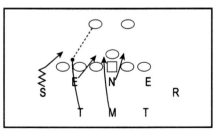

Diagram 6-24

Bronco Sam (Diagram 6-25): This stunt adds Bronco to Sam and also gives the offense the illusion of a four-man strongside rush.

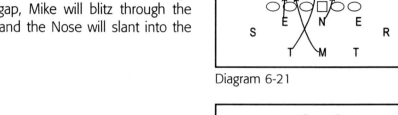

Diagram 6-25

Plus Sam (Diagram 6-26): Plus directs the Stud to creep toward the line of scrimmage and rush from the edge. Because plus is added to Sam, it creates an *overload* strongside *pass rush*. (The term *overload pass rush* means that the defense is rushing enough pass defenders to force the offense to use Max protection, which would require the offense to employ both their tight end and strongside running back to block all of the pass rushers).

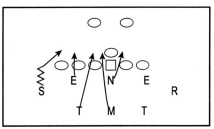

Diagram 6-26

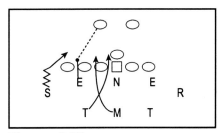

Diagram 6-27

Spy Sax (Diagram 6-27): This stunt adds spy to sax and gives the offense the illusion of a four-man strongside rush.

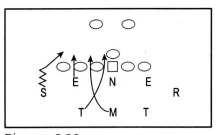

Diagram 6-28

Plus Sax (Diagram 6-28): Plus adds an extra pass rusher (Stud) to sax, making the stunt an overload strongside pass rush scheme.

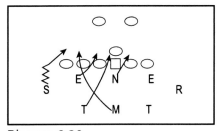

Diagram 6-29

Plus Shark (Diagram 6-29): Plus adds an extra pass rusher (Stud) to shark making the stunt an overload pass rush scheme.

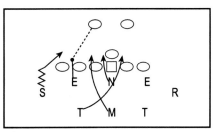

Diagram 6-30

Spy Sex (Diagram 6-30): This stunt adds spy to sex and gives the offense the illusion of a four-man strongside pass rush.

Plus Sex (Diagram 6-31): Plus adds an extra pass rusher (Stud) to sex making the stunt an overload pass rush scheme.

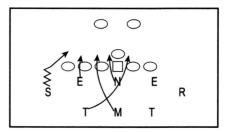

Diagram 6-31

Wham (Diagram 6-32): This stunt is the weakside version of Sam.

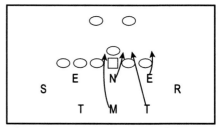

Diagram 6-32

Wax (Diagram 6-33): This stunt is the weakside version of sax.

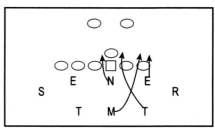

Diagram 6-33

Wolf (Diagram 6-34): This stunt is the weakside version of shark.

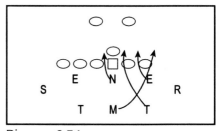

Diagram 6-34

Wex (Diagram 6-35): This stunt is the weakside version of sex.

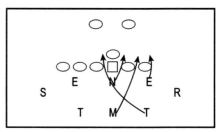

Diagram 6-35

Spy Wham (Diagram 6-36): This stunt is the weakside version of spy Sam.

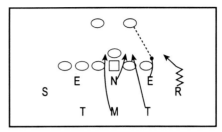

Diagram 6-36

Bronco Wham (Diagram 6-37): This stunt is the weakside version of Bronco Sam.

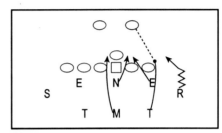

Diagram 6-37

Wham Plus (Diagram 6-38): This stunt is the weakside version of Sam plus.

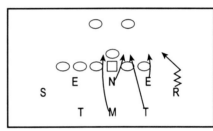

Diagram 6-38

Spy Wax (Diagram 6-39): This stunt is the weakside version of spy sax.

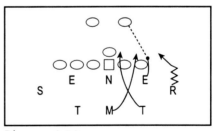

Diagram 6-39

Wax Plus (Diagram 6-40): This stunt is the weakside version of plus sax.

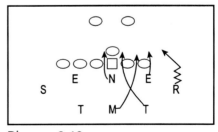

Diagram 6-40

Wolf Plus (Diagram 6-41): This stunt is the weakside version of shark plus.

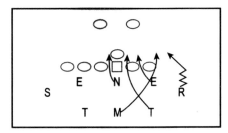

Diagram 6-41

Spy Wex (Diagram 6-42): This stunt is the weakside version of spy sex.

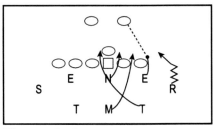

Diagram 6-42

Wex Plus (Diagram 6-43): This stunt is the weakside version of sex plus.

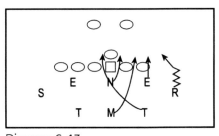

Diagram 6-43

Spy Triple Sax (Diagram 6-44): This stunt merges spy W with spy sax and gives the offense the illusion of an eight-man pass rush.

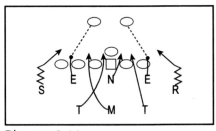

Diagram 6-44

Spy Triple Sex (Diagram 6-45): This stunt merges spy W with spy sex for the purpose of giving the offense the illusion of an eight-man pass rush.

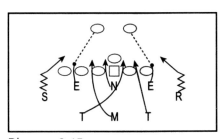

Diagram 6-45

Spy Triple Wax (Diagram 6-46): This stunt is the weakside version of spy triple sax.

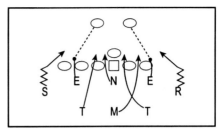

Diagram 6-46

Spy Triple Wex (Diagram 6-47): This stunt is the weakside version of spy triple sex.

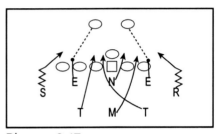

Diagram 6-47

Outlaw (Diagram 6-48): This stunt provides the defense with excellent pressure from the edge, and frees all three stacked linebackers to pursue the ball from an inside-out position.

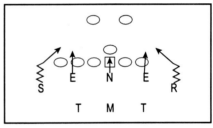

Diagram 6-48

Outlaw Pinch (Diagram 6-49): This stunt not only provides excellent pressure from the edge and frees three stacked linebackers to pursue the ball, but it also fortifies the B gaps. It is a good stunt to go to when traps hurt the defense.

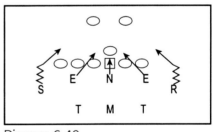

Diagram 6-49

Outlaw Slant (Diagram 6-50): This stunt provides the defense with all of the advantages of outlaw and also enables the three defensive linemen to slant toward the weakside.

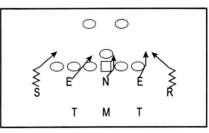

Diagram 6-50

Outlaw Angle (Diagram 6-51): This stunt also provides the defense with all of the advantages of outlaw and also enables the three defensive linemen to slant toward the strongside.

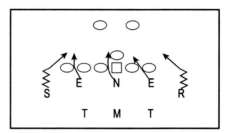

Diagram 6-51

Slant (Diagram 6-52): This stunt provides the defense with all of the advantages of outlaw except weakside pressure from the edge.

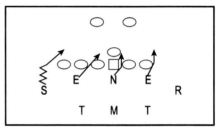

Diagram 6-52

Angle (Diagram 6-53): This stunt provides the defense with all of the advantages of outlaw except weakside pressure from the edge.

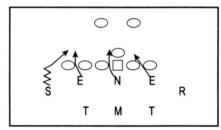

Diagram 6-53

Say (Diagram 6-54): This one-man stunt assigns Stud to rush from the edge.

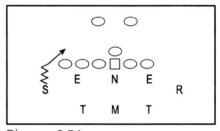

Diagram 6-54

Ray (Diagram 6-55): This one-man stunt assigns Rover to rush from the edge.

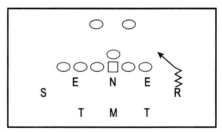

Diagram 6-55

Basic Principles of Stunting

- If stunts are used as an element of surprise and done infrequently, it is important that defenders disguise their intentions.
- If defenders frequently stunt, disguising their intentions may not be as important because they may want to occasionally give the offense a false key by *showing blitz* but then *playing straight* at the snap of the ball. Whatever is decided, it is important that defenders do not establish a pattern, which becomes a key that can be exploited.
- Defenders eyes are one of his most important tools when stunting. To be an effective stunter, a defender must be able to see (on the run) the keys that that will lead him to the ball. Seeing these keys is the first step in being able to read and react to them.
- Unless the stunt is a delayed reaction to a pass, it is critical that defenders are moving, attacking, and penetrating the line of scrimmage at the snap of the ball.
- Defenders must keep their feet moving at all times, which is especially important when they become engaged with a blocker.
- Defenders must use their quickness in an attempt to avoid blockers.
- If the play is a pass, and the defender becomes engaged with a blocker, he must keep his hands inside of the blocker's hands and try to maintain separation from the blocker. He must not look at the passer too soon and lose sight of the blocker. He must first defeat the blocker before he can sack the quarterback. It is important that he has a predetermined pass rush move in mind but is ready to change his move according to the circumstance.
- A defender must take what the blocker gives him and make his move at the appropriate time. He must remember that if he makes his pass rush move too soon that the blocker will have time to recover. On the other hand, if he makes his move too late, he will probably be too close to the blocker and the blocker will be able to get into his body and nullify the defender's charge.
- If possible the defender must try to get the blocker turned one way and then make his move in the opposite direction. Also, the defender should use his forward momentum to manipulate the blocker's momentum. If the blocker's momentum is back, the defender should attack him with a power move and knock him backwards. If his momentum is forward, the defender should use a move that puts the blocker forward and destroys his balance.
- The defender should never leave his feet to bat a ball down. He should get his hands up as the quarterback begins his throwing motion but keep charging toward the quarterback. Too often when a defender jumps up to bat a pass down, the quarterback will duck under, elude the defender, and scramble out of the pocket.
- If the play is a run, the defender should react to his keys and the pressure of blocks as he normally would if he was employing a read technique. Since he has forward momentum to his advantage, the defender should use his hands rather than his forearm when attacking a blocker. He should maintain separation from blockers and not let them get into his legs. If possible, the defender should make the blocker miss him.

- Defenders must keep their bodies under control at all times and try to maintain a low center of gravity. They must provide a small target for blockers.
- Defenders must study their opponent's game films carefully. They must know how potential blockers react and what techniques they favor. They must know blockers' strengths and weaknesses.
- Defenders must study their opponents' eyes as they are getting set at the line of scrimmage. Opponents' eyes will often tell defenders where they are going. They must also study the pressure that opponents put on their down hand when they get into their stances. Defenders can frequently find a player who will give them a pass/run or a directional key by the pressure he puts on his down hand.
- Defenders must study the scouting report, know their opponents' formation, down and distance, and field position tendency. Defenders must use this information to anticipate, but never to guess.
- Defenders must gang tackle, and if possible try to strip the ball out of the ballcarrier's arm. They must never take for granted that a running back or quarterback has been downed. If they arrive at a pile late, defenders must be on the alert for a loose ball.
- Defenders must maintain total intensity from the time the ball is snapped until the whistle is blown.
- Before the snap, defenders should anticipate potential blockers and be prepared to react to these blockers as they penetrate through the line.
- On plays directed toward their side of the line, defenders should make the tackle; on plays directed away from them, they must take the proper angle of pursuit and be in on the tackle. Defenders must always pursue relentlessly and remember that if they are not within five yards of the ball when the whistle blows that they are probably loafing.
- If the backfield action does not indicate flow, defenders must protect their gaps until they find the ball; they must not guess.
- If they are assigned spy or Bronco (cover a back) when they are stunting, defenders must expect that the back will first block and then run a delayed route. They cannot be fooled. They must remember that they must cover the back until the whistle blows no matter what he does.
- The ball is a defender's trigger. When the ball is snapped, the defenders are gone, and must not listen to an opponent's cadence.
- Defenders should rely upon the lines that are marked on the field. The ball—not the lines—establishes the line of scrimmage.

7

Cover 1:
Variations, Stunts, and Adjustments

Cover 1

Cover 1 provides the defense with a five-man pass rush and a free safety who will play centerfield versus pass and back up the defenders aligned in the box who are attempting to stop run. This chapter will present five variations of cover 1: cover 1, cover 1F, cover 1T, cover 1 rob, and cover 1 fire. Although the strengths of cover 1 include the ability to disguise each variation and to pressure the quarterback with a number of different pressure packages from each variation, the main strength of the coverage is its ability to jam receivers at the line and to disrupt the timing of the opponent's passing game. Cover 1 only requires one *island player* when the ball is located on the hash, which it is approximately 80 percent of the time. An *island player* is a pass defender who must cover a pass receiver one-on-one without any help from the free safety. The cover 1 *island player* is referred to as the field corner. All of the other pass defenders will receive deep help from the free safety, enabling the *non-island player* to disrupt the timing of pass routes by jamming receivers and funneling them into the free safety. Diagrams 7-1A through 7-1H illustrate how cover 1 adjusts to eight different offensive formations. Chart 7-1 outlines all of the stunts that might be used with cover 1 and their respective check-offs versus aceback formations. Note that check-offs are not included versus empty formations because empty formations will be dealt with in a separate chapter.

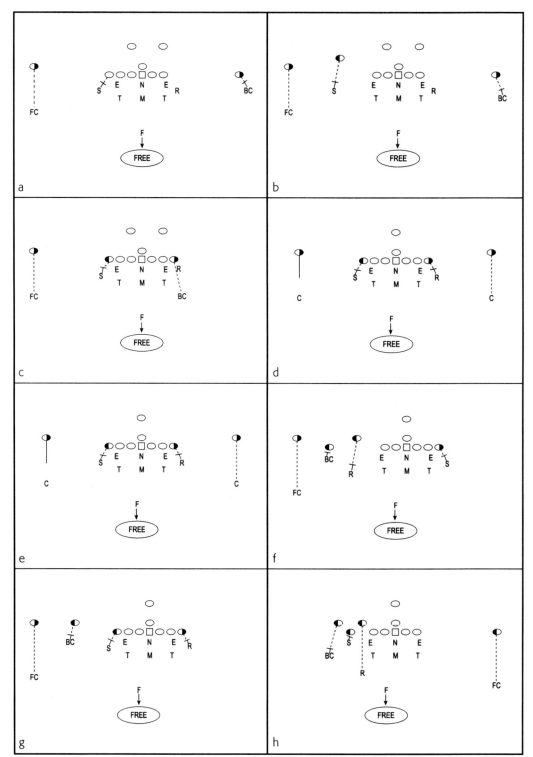

Diagrams 7-1a through 7-1h

Chart 7-1: Cover 1 Stunts and Adjustments

STUNT	PURPOSE	CHECK VERSUS ACE
Tap Mike and Rover cover the two running backs.	Good pass/run stunt that provides the defense with a five-man pass rush and frees Mike and Rover to pursue run.	None necessary. Rover adjusts; Mike covers the aceback.
Nose Tap Mike and Rover cover the two running backs.	Same advantages as tap, plus the added benefit of providing the defense with a strongside twin stunt.	None necessary. Rover adjusts; Mike covers the aceback.
New Tap Mike and Rover cover the two running backs.	Same advantages as tap, plus the added benefit of providing the defense with a weakside twin stunt.	None necessary. Rover adjusts; Mike covers the aceback.
Wham Rover and the strong tandem cover two running backs.	Good pass/run stunt that provides the defense with a five-man pass rush and frees the strong tandem and Rover to pursue run.	None necessary. Rover adjusts; the strong tandem covers the aceback.
Wax Rover and the strong tandem cover two running backs.	Good pass/run stunt that provides the defense with a five-man pass rush and frees the strong tandem and Rover to pursue run.	None necessary. Rover adjusts; the strong tandem covers the aceback.
Wex Rover and the strong tandem cover two running backs.	Good pass/run stunt that provides the defense with a five-man pass rush and frees the strong tandem and Rover to pursue run.	None necessary. Rover adjusts; the strong tandem covers the aceback.
Spy Wham Weak end and the strong tandem cover two running backs.	Good pass/run stunt that provides the defense with a five-man pass and the illusion of a weakside four-man pass rush.	Rover adjusts and alerts the weak end that he does not have to spy; the strong tandem covers the aceback.
Bronco Wham Weak end and the strong tandem cover two running backs.	Good pass/run stunt that provides the defense with a five-man pass and the illusion of a weak side four-man pass rush.	Rover adjusts and alerts the weak tandem that he does not have to spy; the strong tandem covers the aceback.
Spy Wax Weak end and the strong tandem cover two running backs.	Good pass/run stunt that provides the defense with a five-man pass and the illusion of a weak side four-man pass rush.	Rover adjusts and alerts the weak end that he does not have to spy; the strong tandem covers the aceback.
Spy Wex Weak end and the strong tandem cover two running backs.	Good pass/run stunt that provides the defense with five-man pass and the illusion of a weakside four-man pass rush.	Rover adjusts and alerts the weak end that he does not have to spy; the strong tandem covers the aceback.
Ray W Mike and strong tandem cover the two running backs.	Good pass/run stunt that provides the defense with a five-man pass rush and frees Mike and the strong tandem to pursue run.	Rover adjusts and alerts defense that Ray is off. Because the defense is left with only a four-man pass rush, some coaches may wish to check to a stunt that employs five pass rushers.
Ray M Both tandems cover the two running backs.	Good pass/run stunt that provides the defense with a five-man pass rush and frees both tandems to pursue run.	Rover adjusts and alerts defense that Ray is off. Because the defense is left with only a four-man pass rush, some coaches may wish to check to a stunt that employs five pass rushers.
Ray S Mike and the weak tandem cover the two running backs.	Good pass/run stunt that provides the defense with a five-man pass rush and frees both tandems to pursue run.	Rover adjusts and alerts defense that Ray is off. Because the defense is left with only a four-man pass rush, some coaches may wish to check to a stunt that employs five pass rushers.

Cover 1F

Cover 1 enables the defense to apply pressure toward the weakside of an offensive formation. Cover 1F enables the defense to apply pressure to the strongside of an offensive formation. When confronted by an aceback formation, cover 1F will automatically check back to cover 1. The stunt that was originally called in the huddle however, will remain unchanged (unless of course a coach, because of game plan, wishes to change it). Diagrams 7-2A through 7-2H illustrate how cover 1 adjusts to eight different offensive formations. Chart 7-2 outlines all of the stunts that might be used with cover 1F and their respective check-offs versus aceback formations.

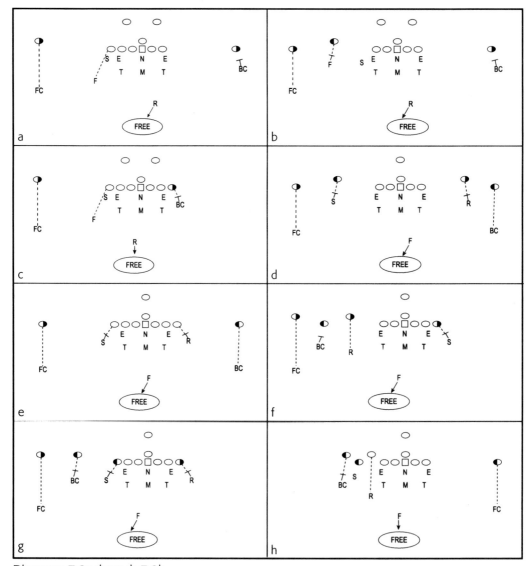

Diagrams 7-2a through 7-2h

Chart 7-2: Cover 1F Stunts and Adjustments

STUNT	PURPOSE	CHECK VERSUS ACE
Tap Mike and Stud cover the two running backs.	Good pass/run stunt that provides the defense with a five-man pass rush and frees Mike and Stud to pursue run.	Secondary checks to cover 1, stunt stays, Mike covers the aceback.
Nose Tap Mike and Stud cover the two running backs.	Same advantages as tap, plus the added benefit of providing the defense with a strongside twin stunt.	Secondary checks to cover 1, stunt stays, Mike covers the aceback.
New Tap Mike and Stud cover the two running backs.	Same advantages as tap, plus the added benefit of providing the defense with a weakside twin stunt.	Secondary checks to cover 1, stunt stays, Mike covers the aceback.
Sam Stud and the Weak tandem cover two running backs.	Good pass/run stunt that provides the defense with a five-man pass rush and frees the weak tandem and Stud to pursue run.	Secondary checks to cover 1, stunt stays, the weak tandem covers the aceback.
Sax Stud and the weak tandem cover two running backs.	Good pass/run stunt that provides the defense with a five-man pass rush and frees the weak tandem and Stud to pursue run.	Secondary checks to cover 1, stunt stays, the weak tandem covers the aceback.
Sex Stud and the weak tandem cover two running backs.	Good pass/run stunt that provides the defense with a five-man pass rush and frees the weak tandem and Stud to pursue run.	Secondary checks to cover 1, stunt stays, the weak tandem covers the aceback.
Spy Sam Strong end and the weak tandem cover two running backs.	Good pass/run stunt that provides the defense with a five-man pass and the illusion of a strongside four-man pass rush.	Secondary checks to cover 1, Stud alerts the weak end that he does not have to spy; the weak tandem covers the aceback.
Bronco Sam Strong end and weak tandem cover two running backs.	Good pass/run stunt that provides the defense with a five-man pass and the illusion of a strongside four-man pass rush.	Secondary checks to cover 1, Stud alerts the strong tandem that he does not have to spy; the weak tandem covers the aceback.
Spy Sax Strong end and the weak tandem cover two running backs.	Good pass/run stunt that provides the defense with a five-man pass and the illusion of a strongside four-man pass rush.	Secondary checks to cover 1, Stud alerts the strong end that he does not have to spy, the weak tandem covers the aceback.
Spy Sex Strong end and the weak tandem cover two running backs.	Good pass/run stunt that provides the defense with a five-man pass and the illusion of a strongside four-man pass rush.	Secondary checks to cover 1, Stud alerts the strong end that he does not have to spy, the weak tandem covers the aceback.
Say W Mike and strong tandem cover the two running backs.	Good pass/run stunt that provides the defense with a five-man pass rush and frees Mike and the strong tandem to pursue run.	Secondary checks to cover 1, Stud alerts the defense that say is off. Because the defense is left with only a four-man pass rush, some coaches may wish to check to a stunt that employs five pass rushers.
Say M Both tandems cover the two running backs.	Good pass/run stunt that provides the defense with a five-man pass rush and frees both tandems to pursue run.	Secondary checks to cover 1, Stud alerts the defense that say is off. Because the defense is left with only a four-man pass rush, some coaches may wish to check to a stunt that employs five pass rushers.
Say S Mike and the weak tandem cover the two running backs.	Good pass/run stunt that provides the defense with a five-man pass rush and frees Mike and the weak tandem to pursue run.	Secondary checks to cover 1, Stud alerts the defense that say is off. Because the defense is left with only a four-man pass rush, some coaches may wish to check to a stunt that employs five pass rushers.

Cover 1T

Cover 1T is only used against offensive formations that employ a tight end. Against formations that do not employ a tight end, always check to cover 1 tap. Other coaches may wish check to something else. When cover 1T is employed, Stud will rush from the edge, Mike will cover the strong back (or aceback), and the strong end will attack the near shoulder of the offensive guard and secure the B gap versus run. Diagrams 7-3A through 7-3H illustrate how cover 1T adjusts to eight different offensive formations. Chart 7-3 outlines all of the stunts that might be used with cover 1T and their respective check-offs versus aceback formations.

Chart 7-3: Cover 1T Stunts and Adjustments

STUNT	PURPOSE	CHECK VERSUS ACE
W Mike and Rover cover the two running backs.	Good pass/run stunt that provides the defense with a five-man pass rush and frees Mike and Rover to pursue run.	None necessary unless no tight end is employed. Versus no tight end, check cover 1 tap.
Spy W Mike and weak end cover the two running backs.	Good pass/run stunt that provides the defense with a five-man pass rush and the illusion of a three-man weakside pass rush.	Rover will alert weakside end that spy is off. W will remain on, and Mike will cover aceback.
New Spy W Mike and weak end cover the two running backs.	Good pass/run stunt that provides the defense with a five-man pass rush and a weakside twin stunt.	Rover will alert weakside end that spy is off. New and W will remain on, and Mike will cover aceback.
Bronco W Mike and weak tandem cover the two running backs.	Good pass/run stunt that provides the defense with a five-man pass rush and the illusion of a three-man weakside pass rush.	Rover will alert weakside tandem that Bronco is off. W will remain on, and Mike will cover aceback.
New Bronco W Mike and weak tandem cover the two running backs.	Good pass/run stunt that provides the defense with a five-man pass rush and a weakside twin stunt.	Rover will alert weakside tandem that Bronco is off. New and W will remain on, and Mike will cover aceback.

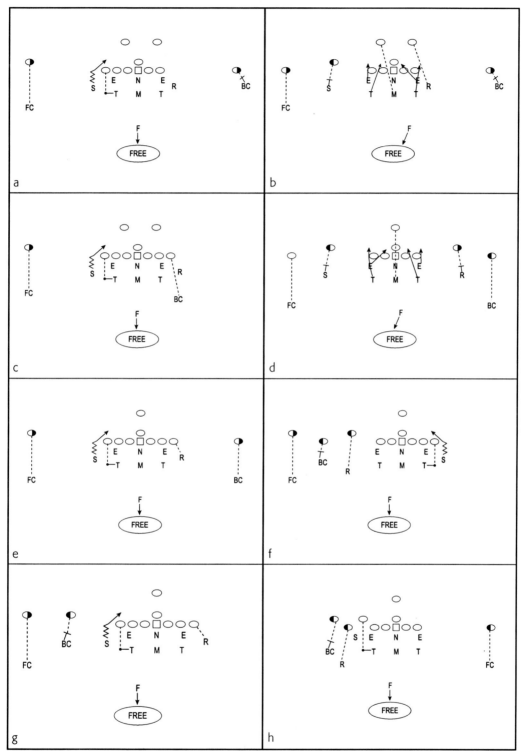

Diagrams 7-3a through 7-3h

Cover 1 Rob

The limitation of cover 1 rob is that it only provides the defense with a four-man pass rush. Its strength is that it provides the defense with an extra cover player to drop to the *hole* (an area directly in front of the center five to seven yards deep) and to aggressively attack crossing routes. Only three stunts will be employed with cover 1 rob: M, W, and S. Cover 1 rob adjustments to various offensive formations are identical to cover 1. Diagram 7-4 illustrates the initial functioning of this coverage versus a drop back pass if M was the stunt called in the huddle. Rover and the strong tandems are assigned to cover the two running backs and Stud is assigned to cover the tight end. The weak tandem is the Robber.

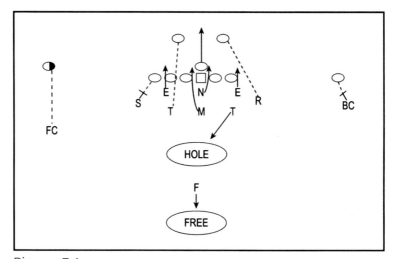

Diagram 7-4

When confronted by a crossing route by the tight end (see Diagram 7-5), Stud will aggressively funnel the tight end into the Robber (the weak tandem) who then jams and covers the tight end. As Stud sees that the weak tandem is beginning to cover the tight end, he will then replace the weak tandem as the Robber and drop to the deep hole (12 to 15 yards deep) and look for a deep crossing pattern such as the dig route.

A full-flow play-action pass alters the assignments of this coverage slightly. Diagram 7-6 illustrates a very common strong side full-flow play-action pass. When confronted by this play, Stud will attack and cover the tight end and the strong tandem will cover the first back out of the backfield (the fullback). The weak tandem will shuffle two steps parallel to the line and then work downhill. The weak tandem is responsible for covering the tailback, and since the tailback is faking a run, the best way to do this is to tackle the tailback. Because Rover has no one to cover, he will replace the weak tandem as the Robber. He will thus drop to the hole, first look for a crossing route by the tight end, and if none occurs, drop to the deep hole and look for a dig pattern.

Diagram 7-7 illustrates how assignments will be altered versus a weakside full-flow play-action pass. Rover will cover the first back out (the fullback), the weak tandem will cover tackle the tailback, Stud will cover the tight end, and the strong tandem will become the Robber.

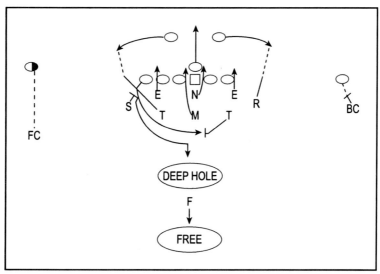

Diagram 7-5

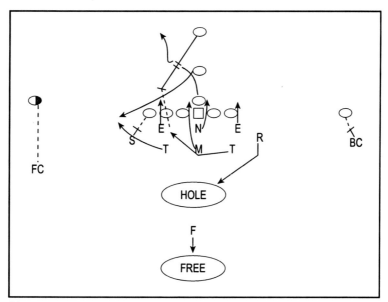

Diagram 7-6

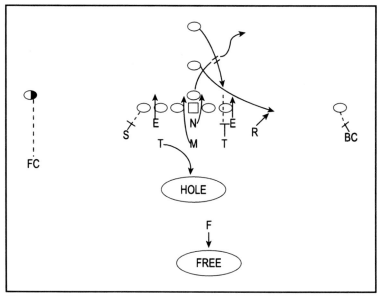

Diagram 7-7

Cover 1 Fire

The formation adjustments for cover 1 fire are identical to cover 1. The following stunts will be used with this coverage: tap (new or nose can be added), Sam, sax, sex, shark, wham, wax, wex, and wolf. Diagram 7-8 illustrates tap being employed with cover 1 fire. In this diagram, Stud, Mike, and Rover drop to three designated areas referred to as Abel, Baker, and Charlie, and combo cover the tight end and two running backs.

Because the specific assignments and techniques have been detailed in two previous Coaches Choice publications (*101 Fire Zone Blitzes and 101 3-5 Stunts*), they will not be repeated in this book; however, a little more detail will be provided to adapting the fire zone blitz to aceback formations. When confronted by an aceback doubles set, a coach has two options. The first option is illustrated in Diagram 7-9. When choosing this option, Rover and Stud will play deep enough to first read the direction of the aceback's course. If the course is toward the Stud, he will banjo cover the aceback and #2 strong with Mike, and Rover will lock onto and single cover #2 weak. Mike will simply read the direction of the aceback's course and *banjo* in that direction.

When the defense chooses the second option, it will employ a four-man pass rush. M, S, and W are the three stunts that are used for this option. Diagram 7-10 illustrates the second option being used with M. In this diagram, both Stud and Rover are employing an outside jam technique, and the two tandems are dropping toward the hook area. Because the aceback is blocking left, Stud and strong tandem will *banjo* #2 strong, and Rover and the weak tandem will *bracket* #2 weak.

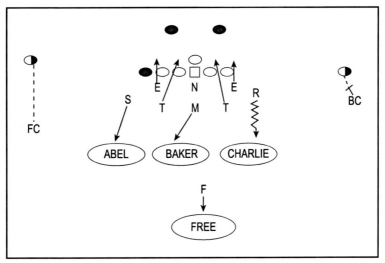

Diagram 7-8

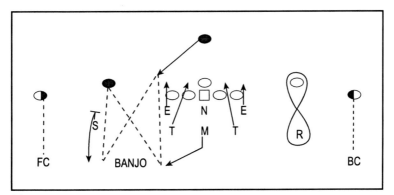

Diagram 7-9

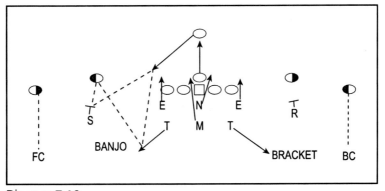

Diagram 7-10

8

Zero Coverage:
Variations, Stunts, and Adjustments

Zero coverage is a man-man coverage that does not employ a free safety. The strength of zero coverage is that it has eight to nine defenders in the vicinity of the box attacking the gaps and penetrating the line of scrimmage. Its weakness is that all secondary defenders are locked on receivers, and none are keying the ball; therefore, if a run breaks the line of scrimmage or a defensive back gets beat deep, chances are good that a touchdown will result. Despite its weakness, zero coverage can cause an offense a lot of problems and has the potential to produce some great defensive plays.

Zero coverage requires the boundary corner to play the same technique as the field corner (inside leverage, seven to eight yards off, etc.). The boundary corner should disguise his intentions whenever possible. The free safety should also disguise his intentions by lining up in the same position that he would line up when playing cover 1, and then stemming to a position that enables him to cover the tight end during cadence. Versus aceback sets, Rover will be the *adjuster*. The defense must therefore check out of any stunt that involves the Rover versus aceback sets. Diagrams 8-1A through 8-1H illustrate how zero coverage adjusts to eight different offensive formations. Chart 8-1 outlines all of the stunts that might be used with zero coverage and their respective check-offs versus aceback formations.

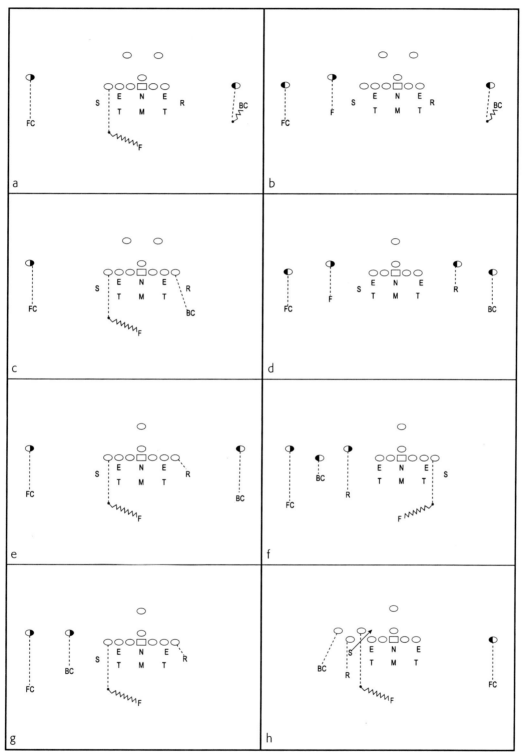

Diagrams 8-1a through 8-1h

Chart 8-1: Zero Coverage Stunts and Adjustments

STUNT	PURPOSE	CHECK VERSUS ACE
Spy Tap Both ends spy the two running backs.	Good pass/run stunt that provides the defense with the illusion of a seven-man pass rush and keeps Mike free to pursue runs from an inside-out position.	Check to say tap. Mike covers the aceback.
Bronco Tap Both tandems spy the two running backs.	Good pass/run stunt that provides the defense with the illusion of a seven-man pass rush and keeps Mike free to pursue runs from an inside-out position.	Check to say tap. Mike covers the aceback.
Bronco Tap Nose (or New) Both tandems spy the two running backs.	Nose and New are good additions to Bronco tap because they enhance the stunt by providing it with the additional advantage of a strongside twin stunt (Nose) or a weakside twin stunt (New).	Check to say tap Nose (or New). Mike covers the aceback.
Spy Triple Tap Both ends spy the two running backs.	Good pass stunt that provides the defense with the illusion of an eight-man pass rush.	Check to say tap. Mike covers the aceback.
Bronco Triple Tap Both tandems spy the two running backs.	Good pass stunt that provides the defense with the illusion of an eight-man pass rush.	Check to say tap. Mike covers the aceback.
Spy Triple Sax Both ends spy the two running backs.	Good pass stunt that provides the defense with the illusion of an eight-man pass rush.	Check to say sax. Weak tandem covers aceback.
Spy Triple Sex Both ends spy the two running backs.	Good pass stunt that provides the defense with the illusion of an eight-man pass rush.	Check to say sex. Weak tandem covers aceback.
Spy Triple Wax Both ends spy the two running backs.	Good pass stunt that provides the defense with the illusion of an eight-man pass rush.	Check to say wax. Strong tandem covers aceback.
Spy Triple Wex Both ends spy the two running backs.	Good pass stunt that provides the defense with the illusion of an eight-man pass rush.	Check to say wex. Strong tandem covers aceback.
Outlaw Both tandems cover the running backs. Mike is free.	Good run stunt that provides excellent pressure from the edge and frees the three inside linebackers to pursue runs from an inside-out position. Good stunt versus an opponent who likes to run outside.	Check to say S, M, W, or Tap because Rover will adjust and weakside pressure from the edge is eliminated.
Outlaw M Both tandems cover the running backs.	Good pass/run stunt that provides excellent pressure from the edge and a six-man pass rush. It also frees the two inside linebackers to pursue runs from an inside-out position.	No check necessary. Rover adjusts.
Outlaw S Mike and the weak tandem cover the running backs.	Good pass/run stunt that provides excellent pressure from the edge and a six-man pass rush.	No check necessary. Rover adjusts.

Chart 8-1: Zero Coverage Stunts and Adjustments (cont.)

STUNT	PURPOSE	CHECK VERSUS ACE
Nose Outlaw S Mike and the weak tandem cover the running backs.	Good pass/run stunt that provides excellent pressure from the edge and a six-man pass rush. The addition of Nose creates a twin stunt that produces a strong side overload.	No check necessary. Rover adjusts.
Outlaw W Mike and the strong tandem cover the running backs.	Good pass/run stunt that provides excellent pressure from the edge and a six-man pass rush. Two inside linebackers are free to pursue runs.	No check necessary. Rover adjusts.
Nose Outlaw W Mike and the weak tandem cover the running backs.	Good pass/run stunt that provides excellent pressure from the edge and a six-man pass rush. The addition of Nose creates a twin stunt that produces a weak side overload.	No check necessary. Rover adjusts.
Outlaw Pinch Both tandems cover the running backs. Mike is free.	Good run stunt that gives the defense aggressive control of the B gaps and provides excellent pressure from the edge. All three inside linebackers are free to pursue run. Good stunt versus an opponent with a strong trap and outside running game.	Check to say W.
M Outlaw Pinch Both tandems cover the running backs.	Provides the defense with all of the advantages of outlaw pinch, plus the additional benefit of a six-man pass rush.	No check necessary. Versus weakside run, the weak tandem will scrape outside and contain.
S Outlaw Pinch Mike and the weak tandem cover the running backs.	Provides the defense with all of the advantages of outlaw pinch, plus the additional benefit of a six-man pass rush.	No check necessary. Versus weakside run, the weak tandem will scrape outside and contain.
S Nose Outlaw Pinch Mike and the weak tandem cover the running backs.	Provides the defense with all of the advantages of outlaw pinch, plus the additional benefit of a six-man pass rush. The addition of Nose creates a twin stunt that produces a strongside overload.	No check necessary. Versus weakside run, the weak tandem will scrape outside and contain.
W Outlaw Pinch Mike and the strong tandem cover the running backs.	Provides the defense with all of the advantages of outlaw pinch, plus the additional benefit of a six-man pass rush.	No check necessary.
W Nose Outlaw Pinch Mike and the strong tandem cover the running backs.	Provides the defense with all of the advantages of outlaw pinch, plus the additional benefit of a six-man pass rush. The addition of Nose creates a twin stunt that produces a weakside overload.	No check necessary.
Outlaw Slant Both tandems cover the running backs. Mike is free.	Good run stunt that enables a defense to slant toward an opponent's tendency, plus providing excellent pressure from the edge. All three inside linebackers are free to pursue run.	No check necessary.

Chart 8-1: Zero Coverage Stunts and Adjustments (cont.)

STUNT	PURPOSE	CHECK VERSUS ACE
Outlaw Slant M Both tandems cover the running backs.	Provides the defense with all of the advantages of outlaw slant, plus the additional benefit of a six-man pass rush.	No check necessary.
Outlaw Slant S Mike and the weak tandem cover the running backs.	Provides the defense with all of the advantages of outlaw slant, plus the additional benefit of a six-man pass rush.	No check necessary.
Outlaw Slant W Mike and the strong tandem cover the running backs.	Provides the defense with all of the advantages of outlaw slant plus the additional benefit of a six-man pass rush.	No check necessary.
Outlaw Angle Both tandems cover the running backs. Mike is free.	Good run stunt that enables a defense to slant toward an opponent's tendency, plus providing excellent pressure from the edge. All three inside linebackers are free to pursue run.	Check to angle W.
Outlaw Angle M Both tandems cover the running backs.	Provides the defense with all of the advantages of outlaw slant, plus the additional benefit of a six-man pass rush.	Check to angle M/W.
Outlaw Angle S Mike and the weak tandem cover the running backs.	Provides the defense with all of the advantages of outlaw slant, plus the additional benefit of a six-man pass rush.	Check to angle S/W.
Outlaw Angle W Mike and the strong tandem cover the running backs.	Provides the defense with all of the advantages of outlaw slant plus, the additional benefit of a six-man pass rush.	No check necessary.

9

Cover 5 and Cover 6

Cover 5

Cover 5 insures the defense of a weakside overload pass rush. Cover 5 is a variation of zero coverage. Cover 5 is easily disguised as cover 1. Stud will cover the tight end, and the free safety will cover the weakside running back. The free safety is the *adjuster* to aceback formations. Diagrams 9-1A through 9-1H illustrate how cover 5 adjusts to eight different offensive formations. Chart 9-1 outlines all of the stunts that might be used with cover 5 and their respective check-offs versus aceback formations.

Cover 5 also enables the defense to pressure the offense with a weakside free safety blitz. When a free safety blitz is desired, the term *flash* is added to cover 5. Flash should be used with spy wham, Bronco wham, spy wax, or spy wex. Diagram 9-2 illustrates *Bronco wham–5 Flash*.

Since the free safety is the cover 5 *adjuster* versus aceback sets, the defense will simply check out of the free safety blitz and check to a plus weakside overload of whatever stunt had been originally called in the huddle. Therefore, if Bronco wham–5 Flash was called in the huddle and the offense was to line up in an aceback set, the free safety would adjust and the defense would check to wham plus.

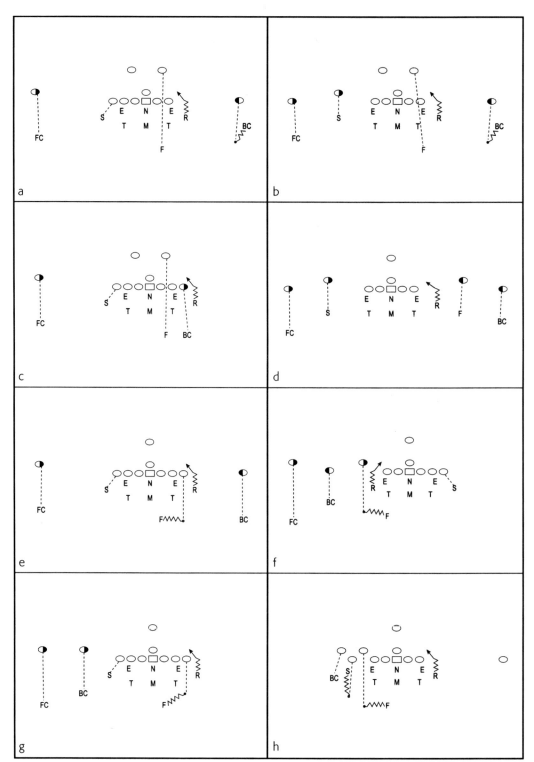

Diagrams 9-1a through 9-1h

Chart 9-1: Cover 5 Stunts and Adjustments

STUNT	PURPOSE	CHECK VERSUS ACE
Wham Plus The free safety and strong tandem cover the two running backs.	Good stunt versus pass and weakside runs; provides the defense with a four-man weakside overload pass rush, and keeps the free safety and strong tandem free to pursue runs.	None necessary. The free safety adjusts and the strong tandem covers the aceback.
Wax Plus The free safety and strong tandem cover the two running backs.	Good stunt versus pass and weakside runs; provides the defense with a four-man weakside overload pass rush, and keeps the free safety and strong tandem free to pursue runs.	None necessary. The free safety adjusts and the strong tandem covers the aceback.
Wex Plus The free safety and strong tandem cover the two running backs.	Good stunt versus pass and weakside runs; provides the defense with a four-man weakside overload pass rush, and keeps the free safety and strong tandem free to pursue runs.	None necessary. The free safety adjusts and the strong tandem covers the aceback.
Wolf Plus The free safety and strong tandem cover the two running backs.	Good stunt versus pass and weakside runs; provides the defense with a four-man weakside overload pass rush and keeps the free safety and strong tandem free to pursue runs.	None necessary. The free safety adjusts and the strong tandem covers the aceback.

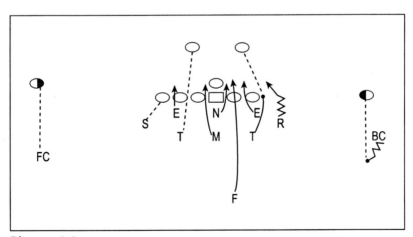

Diagram 9-2

Cover 6

Cover 6 insures the defense of a strong side overload pass rush. Like cover 5, cover 6 is a variations of zero coverage. Cover 6 is easily disguised as cover 1F. The free safety will cover the tight end, and Rover will cover the strongside running back. The Rover is the *adjuster* to aceback formations. Diagrams 9-3A through 9-3H illustrate how cover 6 adjusts to eight different offensive formations. Chart 9-2 outlines all of the stunts that might be used with cover 6 and their respective check-offs versus aceback formations.

Like cover 5, cover 6 also enables the defense to pressure the offense with a secondary blitz. In this case, Rover will be blitzing from the free safety position. This blitz is referred to as *Rumble*. 6 Rumble should be used with spy Sam, Bronco Sam, spy sax, or spy sex. Diagram 9-4 illustrates *spy Sam–6 Rumble*.

Since Rover is the cover 6 adjuster versus aceback sets, the defense will follow a similar procedure to the one it used with cover 5 when it is confronted by an aceback formation. Therefore, if spy Sam–Rumble was called in the huddle and the offense were to line up in an aceback set, Rover would adjust and the defense would check to Sam plus.

Chart 9-2: Cover 6 and Adjustments

STUNT	PURPOSE	CHECK VERSUS ACE
Sam Plus Rover and the weak tandem cover the two running backs.	Good stunt versus pass and strongside runs; provides the defense with a four-man strongside overload pass rush, and keeps the weak tandem and Rover free to pursue runs.	None necessary. Rover adjusts and the weak tandem covers the aceback.
Sax Plus Rover and the weak tandem cover the two running backs.	Good stunt versus pass and strongside runs; provides the defense with a four-man strongside overload pass rush, and keeps the weak tandem and Rover free to pursue runs.	None necessary. Rover adjusts and the weak tandem covers the aceback.
Sex Plus Rover and the weak tandem cover the two running backs.	Good stunt versus pass and strongside runs; provides the defense with a four-man strongside overload pass rush, and keeps the weak tandem and Rover free to pursue runs.	None necessary. Rover adjusts and the weak tandem covers the aceback.
Shark Plus Rover and the weak tandem cover the two running backs.	Good stunt versus pass and strongside runs; provides the defense with a four-man strongside overload pass rush, and keeps the weak tandem and Rover free to pursue runs.	None necessary. Rover adjusts and the weak tandem covers the aceback.

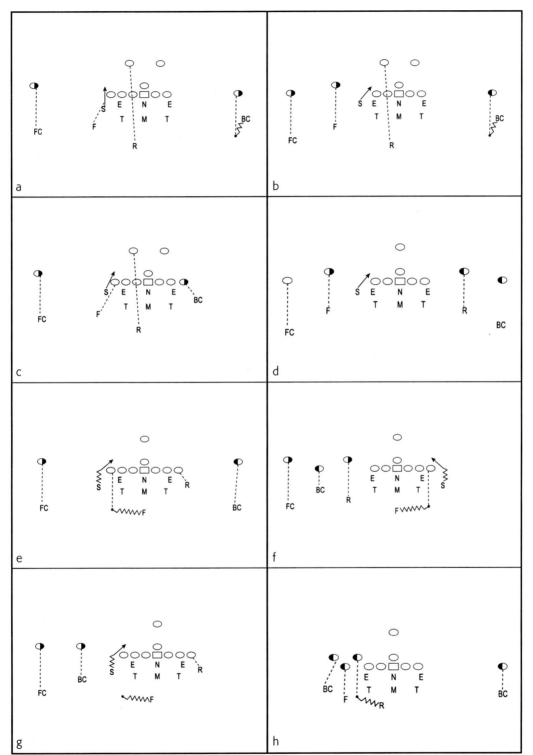

Diagrams 9-3a through 9-3h

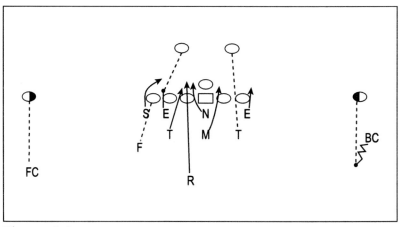

Diagram 9-4

10

Cover 3:
Variations, Adjustments, Stunts, and Pattern Reads

Cover 3 is a three-deep, four-underneath zone coverage. The following are some of the weaknesses and strengths for this zone coverage.

Weaknesses of a Zone Coverage

- Horizontal seams between each zone.
- Each zone can be *high-lowed* (vertically stretched) by putting one receiver at the bottom of the zone and another one at the top.
- Linebackers can be prevented from dropping to their assigned zone, or momentarily frozen with run action fakes.
- Most zone defenses feature a four-man pass rush, which is usually predictable, and frequently does not exert enough pressure on the quarterback.
- Many zone coverages do not collision pass routes and disrupt the timing between the quarterback and his receivers.

Strengths of a Zone Coverage

- Because defensive backs are keying quarterback (along with the receivers), they can break on the quarterback's throw, which often results in more interceptions.
- Defensive backs are seldom "isolated on an island." Another defender is usually providing help.
- It is usually more difficult for the offense to create a mismatch.
- The defense is less likely to give up the big play while in a zone coverage.
- It is much more difficult for the offense to create "rubs" (a legal version of the old "pick" play).
- If the quarterback is accustomed to seeing mostly man coverage, it may surprise him; furthermore, it may disrupt his play calling.

Base Variation of Cover 3

A number of simple variations enhance this base version of cover 3. Use the following stunts with this base version of cover 3: S, M, and W. The base version and its adjustments (when used with M) is illustrated in Diagrams 10-1A through 10-1H. Note the adjustments that are being made versus the three trips formations in Diagrams 10-1F, G, and H.

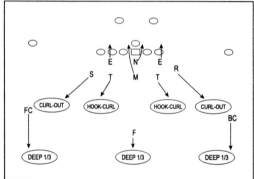

Diagram 10-1a

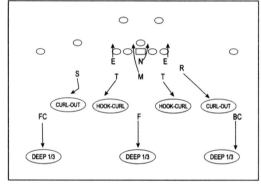

Diagram 10-1b

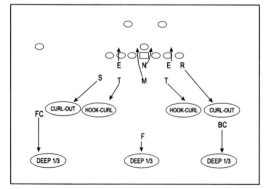

Diagram 10-1c

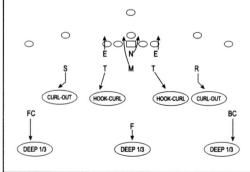

Diagram 10-1d

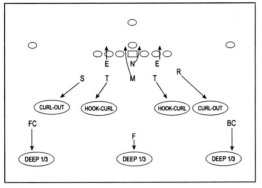

Diagram 10-1e

Diagram 10-1f

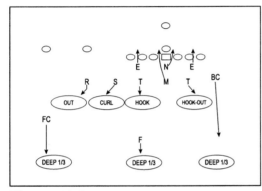

Diagram 10-1g

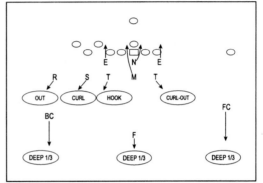

Diagram 10-1h

Zone Drop Pattern Reads

Having a defender not only drop to a spot on the field, but also giving him specific keys and having him read and react to not only the quarterback but also his specific keys is extremely important. The following pattern read guidelines (versus a standard pro formation) will assist defenders who are dropping into one of the cover 3 zones.

Strong Hook-Curl Drop

Defender drops to a depth of 12 to 15 yards into the strong hook zone, and keys #2 (the tight end). If #2 runs a vertical route, he stays in the hook and collisions #2. If #2 releases into the flats, the defender sprints to the curl and looks for #1 (the flanker) to run a curl or a post. If #2 runs inside and across his face, the defender tries to collision #2, and then looks for another receiver to run a crossing route into his zone.

Weak Hook-Curl Drop

Defender opens up and drops to a depth of 12 to 15 yards into the weak hook zone, and keys #2 (the weakside halfback). If #2 runs a vertical route, the defender stays in the hook and collision #2. If #2 releases into the flats, the defender sprints to the curl and looks for #1 (the split end) to run a curl or a post. If #2 runs inside and across his face, the defender tries to collision #2 and then looks for another receiver to run a crossing route into his zone.

Strong Curl-Out Drop

Defender opens up and drops to a depth of 10 to 12 yards. His aiming point is three yards inside of where #1 (the flanker) lined up. He keys #1. If #1 runs an out, the defender tries to get into the throwing lane and get a piece of the ball. If #1 runs a curl or a post, the defender stays inside of #1's pattern and checks #2 (the tight end). If #2 runs an out, the defender must release from #1's curl or post when #2 crosses his face. If #1 runs a vertical route, the defender sinks and checks #2 and #3.

Weak Curl-Out Drop

Defender opens up and drops to a depth of 10 to 12 yards. His aiming point is three yards inside of where #1 (the split end) lined up. He keys #1. If #1 runs an out, the defender tries to get into the throwing lane and get a piece of the ball. If #1 runs a curl or a post, the defender stays inside of his pattern and check #2 (the weakside halfback). If #2 runs an out, the defender must release from #1's curl or post when #2 crosses his face. If #1 runs a vertical route, the defender sinks and checks #2.

Deep Outside 1/3 Drop

The field and boundary corner are responsible for covering this area. They must see both #1 and #2 as they back pedal. The corners will line up eight to nine yards from #1. They must be deeper than any receiver in their zone. If #1 runs a short or intermediate route, the corner will look for #2 to threaten the defender in his zone. He must communicate with the backers on the type of route. For example, if #1 runs an out, the cornerback should be yelling "out-out" to the backer and looking back at #2 to threaten him deep. If #2 runs a short or intermediate route, the corner must control the speed of his backpedal in order to break on the ball. If #1 runs a vertical route, the corner will maintain a cushion of three to four yards. If #1 runs a post, the corner stays on the receiver's outside hip and maintains a sufficient cushion.

Deep Middle 1/3 Drop

The free safety will line up at a mid point between #1 strong and #1 weak. His normal depth should be between 12 and 15 yards deep. The free safety must never allow any receiver in his zone to beat him deep. He must be ready to break on any routes in his zone. He will key #2's release. If it is vertical, the defender must be in a position to cover it. If #2 goes flat, the free safety will look for #1 on either side to run a post. It is vital that the free safety communicates with the linebackers.

Cover 3 Variations

The major weakness of pattern reading is that it does not account for #3 strong versus a two back formation. The first variation, 3 Max (see Diagram 10-2), remedies this weakness. 3 Max is also a good check-off versus trips or an empty set.

The next two variations are implemented from a four-deep look. Because the ball is located on or near the hash approximately 80 percent of the time, these variations—sky (see Diagram 10-3) and 3 Cloud (see Diagram 10-4)—enable you to zone the field more realistically. Only use these variations when the ball is on the hash, and with the following stunts: angle, S, M, and W. The last variation—3D (see Diagram 10-5)—disguises cover 3 from a four-deep look. In every other aspect, 3D is identical to cover 3.

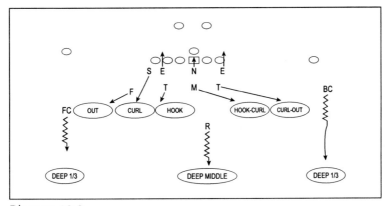

Diagram 10-2

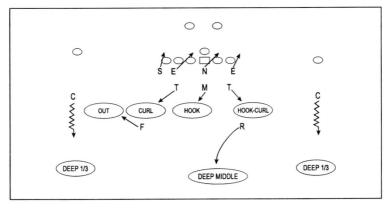

Diagram 10-3

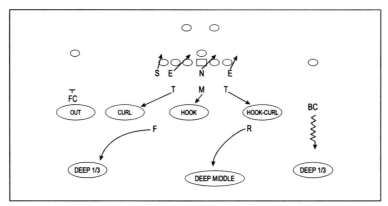

Diagram 10-4

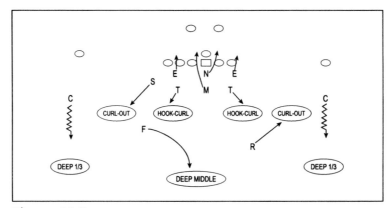

Diagram 10-5

11

Cover 2:
Man and Zone

The strength of cover 2 (man or zone) is that it enables defenders to jam receivers at the line of scrimmage and thus redirect pass routes and disrupt the timing between the quarterback and the receivers. This book employs three variations of cover 2: cover 20, cover 24, and cover 25.

Cover 20

Cover 20 is this book's version of cover 2 man. When this variation is used, you will employ one of these stunts: M, S, or W. Because the weak tandem is the adjuster versus aceback, you will check out of W and into either M or S when confronted by this type of formation. Diagrams 11-1A through 11-1H illustrate the adjustments for cover 20.

The following are the assignments, reads, and responsibilities of defenders assigned to drop to the deep half of the field:

- Defender gains depth; he must cover half of the field and keep all receivers in front of himself.

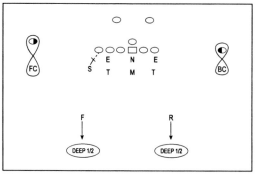

Diagram 11-1a

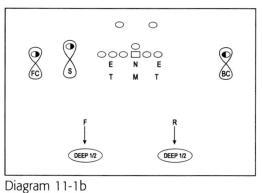

Diagram 11-1b

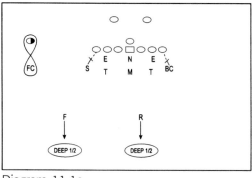

Diagram 11-1c

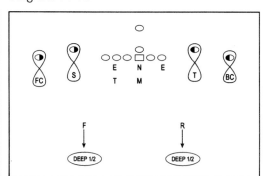

Diagram 11-1d

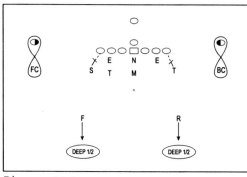

Diagram 11-1e

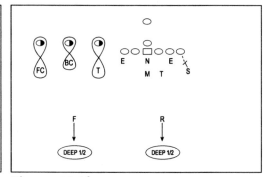

Diagram 11-1f

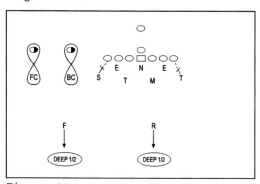

Diagram 11-1g

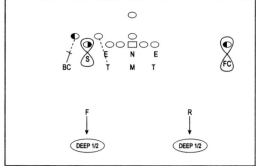

Diagram 11-1h

- He must communicate routes to defenders dropping into the underneath zones.

- He reads #1 and #2. He will work toward and maintain an adequate cushion on the deepest receiver.

- If both receivers go deep, the defender moves outside of #2 so that he will be able to break to #1. Gaining depth is vital. The defender should favor the shortest throw for the quarterback, but stay deep enough to react to both receivers.

- If #2 releases into the flats, the defender gains width and depth and puts himself in a position to react to the route being run by #1.

- If #2 releases inside, the defender gains width and looks first to #1 and then to a deep crossing route.

The defenders assigned to jam and cover wide receivers will use the following techniques:

- Defender lines up two yards deep on the inside eye of the receiver. His feet should be shoulder-width apart and parallel. His eyes should be focused on the receiver's midsection.

- Defender will collision all inside releases by taking a lateral step (about six inches) and punching the receiver's sternum with his inside arm. It is important that he does not lunge or become overly aggressive when carrying out this technique. It is also important that the defender only punch the receiver backwards. If he punches the receiver right or left, he will be helping the receiver gain separation. As he punches, the defender opens his near hip and sprints to the cut-off point. It is vital that the defender takes the proper angle on the receiver's route as he attempts to cut him off. Keying the receiver's near number will help him accomplish this task.

- Defender concentrates on the receiver and stays within a yard of the receiver as he covers his route. He must not peek at back at the quarterback; the defender will find the ball when the receiver looks for it. The defender plays the blur of the ball.

- Versus an outside release, the defender mirrors the receiver's release. He will not jam the receiver; instead, he will work to the cut-off point and attempt to pin the receiver into the boundary. The defender will not react as quickly to outside releases as he does to inside releases.

- If the receiver counter releases, the defender will have already opened his hips. It is therefore vital that he immediately whips his head, turns, and sprints to the cut-off point.

- In most situations, you will not ask the defender to trail the receiver. However, against teams that employ a lot of comeback routes a trail technique is the most appropriate. When trailing, the defender should be one yard inside and one yard behind the receiver.

Cover 25

Cover 25 is this book's version of a two-deep, five-under zone. Diagrams 11-2A through 11-2H illustrate the adjustments and zones to be covered when cover 25 is used. Use the same exact stunts and check-offs for this coverage as for cover 20. The defenders assigned to cover the deep half of the will also use the same techniques and reads as they did with cover 20. The linebackers dropping into the underneath zones will employ the same pattern reads and techniques as they did in cover 3. The only players who need to alter their technique are the cornerbacks who are assigned to jam and funnel the wide receivers and then cover the out zones. The following are the techniques and responsibilities of these defenders:

- Defender jams #1, stays on the receiver's outside shoulder, and funnels him inside. The defender must not allow #1 an outside release.

- If #1 runs a vertical route, the defender continues to funnel the receiver's pattern inside. The defender should also continue to gain depth as long as there is no immediate threat in the flats.

- As he funnels #1 inside, the defender must see the release of #2.

- If #2 releases short into the flat, the defender will not react to his pattern until #2 crosses his face.

- If #2 runs the wheel route, the defender will collision and run with #2.

- If #2 runs a vertical or crossing route, the defender stays with #1 unless threatened by #3. If #3 releases into the flats, he must be in a position to rally up.

Cover 24

Cover 24 is this book's two-deep, four-underneath zone. Although the underneath coverage is not as sound as it is with cover 25, the amount of pressure that you are able to exert upon the quarterback should offset this weakness. The following stunts can be used with cover 24: Sam, sax, sex, shark, tap, snake and M snake. The linebackers who are not involved in these stunts will drop hook-curl. Diagrams 11-3A and 11-3B illustrate how cover 24 (using a Sam stunt) functions versus a both two-back and aceback formation.

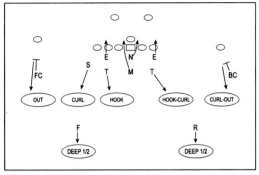

Diagram 11-2a

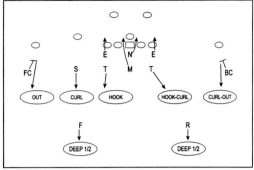

Diagram 11-2b

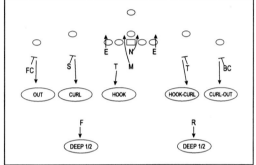

Diagram 11-2c

Diagram 11-2d

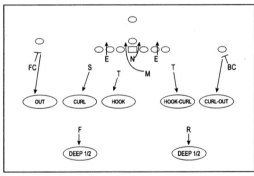

Diagram 11-2e

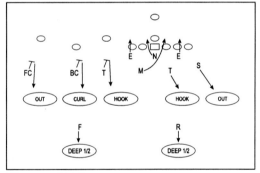

Diagram 11-2f

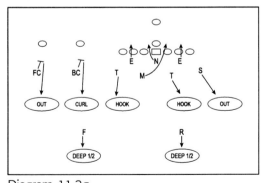

Diagram 11-2g

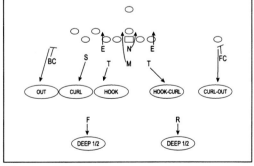

Diagram 11-2h

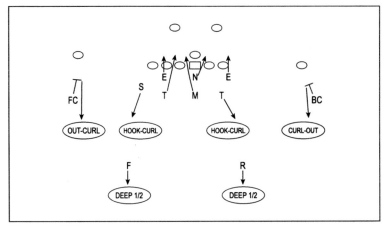

Diagram 11-3a

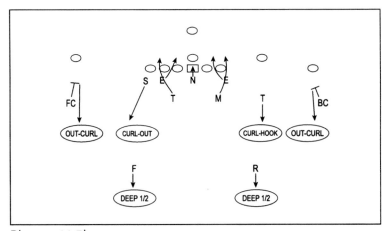

Diagram 11-3b

12

Creating an Impenetrable 3-3-5 Goal Line Defense

The goal line package that will be presented in this chapter not only empowers a defense to load up the box with as many defenders as possible, but it is also simple, flexible, and functional. Diagram 12-1 illustrates the goal line defense versus a standard pro formation. Note the changes that have occurred:

- The strong tandem has moved to a 7 technique. He will line up in a low parallel stance on the inside eye of the tight end. He will jam the tight end by stepping with his outside foot and attacking the tight end's inside number with the heel of his outside hand. After jamming the tight end, he will immediately get his eyes back inside. The strong tandem's key is the tight end to the near back. When flow is toward him, the strong tandem is responsible for controlling the C gap. He must hang tough in the C gap and not be crushed inside or driven backwards by the tight end. He will take on all other blocks (near back or pulling linemen) with his outside forearm (*wrong arm*). Versus pass, he will contain the quarterback (unless coverage assignment differs), and when flow is away, the strong tandem will chase the play along the heel line and check for counter, cutback, or reverse.

- The weak tandem has assumed a rush end position one-and-a-half yards outside of the offensive tackle. At the snap of the ball, the weak tandem will penetrate to the heel line of the offensive tackle. He must control the C gap and cannot be hooked or pushed outside by the offensive tackle. When the offensive tackle blocks inside, the defender will close inside and either chase along the heel line when flow is away, or wrong arm any blocks by a pulling lineman or running back when flow is toward him. Versus pass, the weak tandem will contain the quarterback. When confronted by two tight ends, the weak tandem's techniques and responsibilities are identical to those of the strong tandem, and versus no tight ends, the strong tandem will play as the weak tandem does.

- Stud will line up on the outside eye of the tight end in a good low hitting position. He will jam the tight end by stepping with his inside foot and attack the tight end's outside number with the heel of his inside hand. Stud will key the tight end to the near back. He will maintain an outside relationship on the tight end. If the tight end tries to hook Stud, he will control the tight end's outside shoulder and defeat his block; if the tight end attempts to release outside, Stud will slide outside with the tight end and deny him an outside release. Stud will wrong arm all blocks by a running back or pulling lineman. When flow is toward him, Stud will control the D gap. When flow is away he will sink back and check for counter, reverse and tight end throwback. Versus pass, Stud will cover the tight end. (unless coverage assignment differs). Rover will assume the same assignment and responsibilities as Stud versus double tight ends.

- Both ends will line up in a 3 technique. They will aggressively attack the offensive guards' outside shoulders with a violent hand shiver. They will attempt to knock the guards backwards. The ends are responsible for controlling the B gaps; the guards can never hook them. They will squeeze the A gaps with the guards' bodies when confronted by turn out blocks. If the guard blocks inside, the end will wrong arm the trap. When flow is away, the ends will collapse the backside and pursue along the heel line.

- Mike will move closer to the line versus two and three back sets. Versus aceback sets, Mike will replace the Rover.

- The free safety and Rover will line up four to five yards deep, on the outside shoulder of the offensive tackles. Rover will adjust to aceback sets, but the free safety will maintain his original position. Versus flow toward them, these defenders are responsible for containment. They should take two steps parallel to the line of scrimmage and then quickly scrape outside. They will attack all lead bocks with an inside forearm rip and strive to keep their outside arms and legs back and free. When flow is away, these defenders will take two steps parallel to the line of scrimmage, checking first for counter or reverse, and then working downhill to pursue the ball from an inside-out position. Versus pass, their assignments are predicated upon the offensive set.

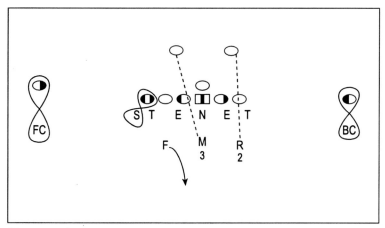
Diagram 12-1

Diagrams 12-2A through 12-2H illustrate how the defense adjusts to eight of the most common offensive formations that one might encounter in the red zone. The scope of this book does not permit a complete and detailed analysis of how the 3-3-5 goal line defense functions against every play that it may encounter, but an explanation of the key coaching points for defending the following offensive plays may help the reader gain an overall understanding of the defense.

Isolation (Diagram 12-3A)

- Stud will jam the tight end, watch for a tight end delay, and maintain outside leverage on the tailback.
- Free safety will attack the fullback with an inside forearm rip as close to the line of scrimmage as possible. He will keep his outside foot back and maintain outside leverage on the ball.
- Mike will immediately work downhill and tackle the ball carrier from an inside-out position.

Sweep (Diagram 12-3B)

- Stud and strong tandem will control their respective blockers' outside shoulders and secure their primary gap of responsibility before pursuing the ball.
- Free safety will scrape outside, rip through the fullback's block with his inside forearm and either force the ballcarrier wide and deep or back inside. The free safety's primary responsibility is containment.
- Mike and Rover will work downhill and pursue the ball from an inside-out position. Their primary responsibility is cutback.

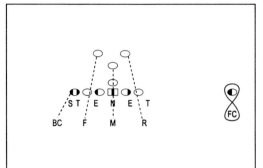

Diagram 12-2a

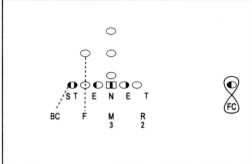

Diagram 12-2b

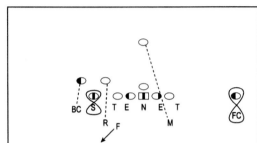

Diagram 12-2c

Diagram 12-2d

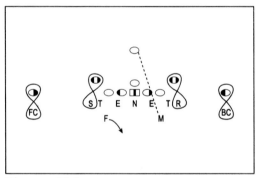

Diagram 12-2e

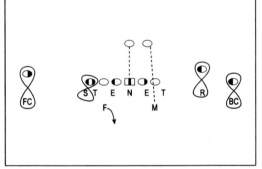

Diagram 12-2f

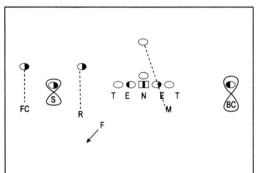

Diagram 12-2g

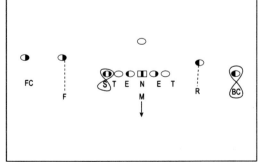

Diagram 12-2h

Veer (Diagram 12-3C)

- Stud will jam the tight end, defeat his block, and play quarterback to pitch. Stud must be prepared to cover the tight end if he should release on a delayed pass route.
- After jamming the tight end, the strong tandem must get his eyes back inside and immediately attack the dive back at the mesh point.
- Mike must work downhill, and tackle the quarterback from an inside-out position.
- Rover must work downhill, and tackle the dive back from an inside-out position.

Full-Flow Play-Action Pass (Diagram 12-3D)

- Stud will jam and cover the tight end.
- The strong tandem will jam the tight end, ricochet off the tailback's block, and contain the quarterback.
- Free safety will scrape outside and cover the fullback.
- Mike will work downhill and check the tailback for a delay route.
- Rover will shuffle down the line and rob any crossing routes.

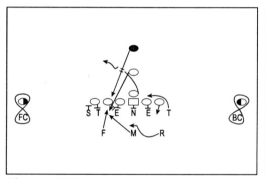

Diagram 12-3a

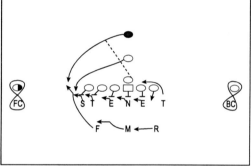

Diagram 12-3b

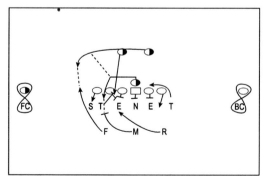

Diagram 12-3c

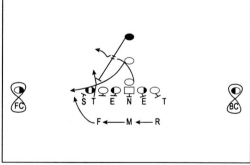

Diagram 12-3d

Speed Option–Aceback Formation (Diagram 12-3E)

- Stud will jam the tight end, and immediately tackle the quarterback. He should drive his face mask through the quarterback's pitch arm.
- Strong tandem should fight through the tight end's block and attempt to gain penetration into the backfield. Hopefully he will be able to get a hand on the quarterback. If not, he should be able to force the quarterback to redirect his course downhill.
- Free safety will scrape outside and tackle the pitchback.
- Mike will shuffle laterally, work downhill, and pursue the ball from an inside-out position.

Empty Set Passing Game (Diagram 12-3F)

- Using this formation, many teams will run a quarterback draw in the red zone. If this were the tendency, the tandems might contain rush and put Mike in a one-on-one situation with the quarterback (not illustrated). If this were the case, the Nose might also be put on a slightly slower check-quarterback rush technique. Of course, this formation would leave five of the pass defenders with one-on-one coverage responsibilities, which is quite risky.
- An alternative method is the illustrated tactic. Employing M attempts to immediately flush the quarterback out of the pocket or his intended draw tract.
- The ends have the very important function of getting their hands on the guards, pulling the guards outside, and making it difficult for the guards to protect the A gaps. Once they are sure the play is a pass, the ends will then work outside and contain the quarterback.
- The tandems will first check run, but as they read pass, they will drop inside of their nearest receiver and rob crossing routes. Doing so achieves the benefits of *double robber* coverage.

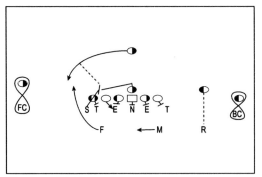

Diagram 12-3e

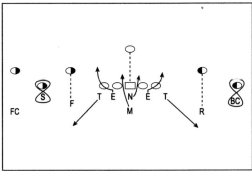

Diagram 12-3f

13

Defending Empty Sets

An empty set is defined as any formation with no backs (except the quarterback) in the backfield. Empty sets are not new. Dutch Meyer successfully used them when he was head coach of TCU during the late 1940s and early 1950s. He even wrote a book (*Spread Formation Football*) about an offense that employed empty sets as its staple in 1952. In recent years, empty sets have been revamped, and now almost every high school and college team uses some form of this formation.

Unless you are playing a team that uses empty sets almost exclusively, you will have a special check-off (sometimes two or three) whenever you encounter the formation. For example, you will *check red*, or *check blue* whenever a team lines up or motions to an empty set. Versus a team that uses this formation exclusively, you will probably devise a game plan that employs three or four different coverages that are enhanced with variety of stunt tactics and coverage disguises.

A number of schools of thought have emerged on how to best defense an empty set. Some coaches believe that the best defense is to rush three and drop eight; others believe in *sending the house*. The game plans discussed here depend upon a number of factors such as the down and distance situation, the mobility of the quarterback, how the running game has or has not been incorporated into the offense, and how the defensive back's speed and skill matches up with that of the wide receivers. Like any other predominately passing attack, try to incorporate the following defensive tactics into your game plan:

- Disguise coverages and confuse the quarterback's reads.
- Collision receivers and disrupt the timing of pass routes.
- Pressure the quarterback so that he must throw off balance, make hurried throws, and bad decisions.
- Confuse the quarterback's hot reads so that he ends up dumping the ball off to receivers in long passing situations.
- The following are some of the coverages and tactics to use versus empty sets.

Cover 3

Two variations of cover 3 will be used. The first variation drops eight and rushes three (see Diagram 13-1). The big questions that a coach must ask when contemplating this variation are first, will the defense be able to stop the quarterback draw (if the quarterback is mobile), and second, will the pass rush be adequate to pressure the quarterback?

The second variation of cover 3 rushes four and drops seven (see Diagram 13-2). It should be used with and M stunt. This variation provides a better pass rush, but may be vulnerable to high-low combination pass routes that isolate the weak tandem, responsible for covering the curl-out zone. To remedy this problem, you can sometimes play a hybrid version of cover 3 and lock the boundary corner on #1 and the weak tandem on #2.

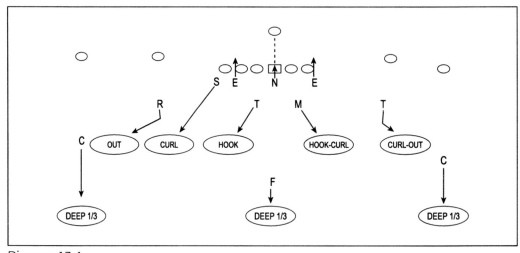

Diagram 13-1

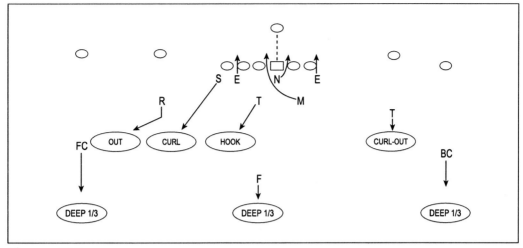

Diagram 13-2

Cover 2 (Man and Zone)

Cover 2 man (see Diagram 13-3) provides a four-man pass rush, enables disruption of the timing between the quarterback and receivers by having the defenders who are locked on receivers use a jam technique, and supplies these defenders with excellent help over the top. Its limitation is that there may not be enough defenders in the box to constrain a mobile quarterback who has a complete repertoire of running plays at his disposal. Cover 2 zone (see Diagram 13-4) has the same basic strengths and limitations as cover 2 man, but the threat of five vertical pass routes should make coaches cautious about using this variation very much.

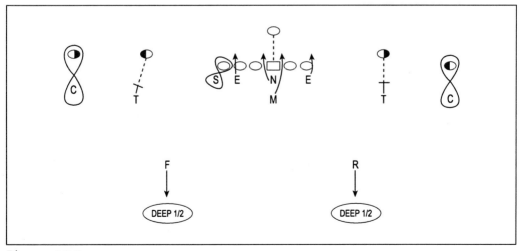

Diagram 13-3

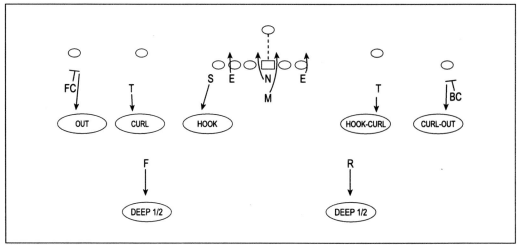

Diagram 13-4

Cover 1

This variation supplies a five-man pass rush that should provide plenty of pressure on the quarterback. Another advantage is that at least three defenders (Stud, Rover, and the weak tandem) are jamming receivers and funneling them into the free safety. If the ball is on the hash, the boundary corner will also be able to employ a jam and funnel technique. This variation is good versus a mobile quarterback.

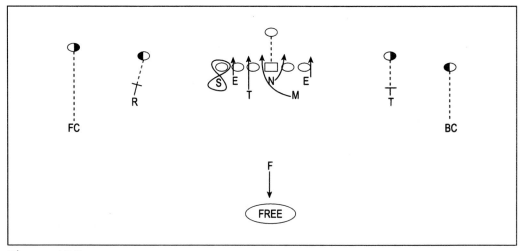

Diagram 13-5

Zero Coverage

When this tactic is employed, the defense is truly sending the house–which may result in a very big play for either the offense or the defense! Use this variation at the goal. To prevent picks, play the coverage players at different levels. Diagram 13-6 illustrates a triple tap stunt that gives great inside pressure, and Diagram 13-7 shows the same stunt being disguised from a cover 2 look. The second variation provides excellent pressure from the edge.

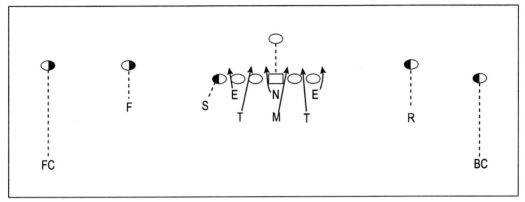

Diagram 13-6

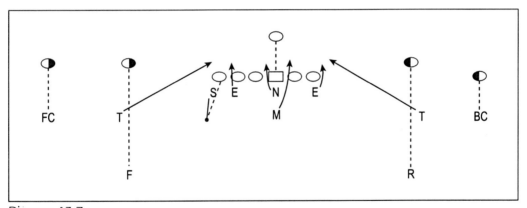

Diagram 13-7

14

Organizing a
3-3-5 Practice Schedule

The purpose of this brief and final chapter is to present some ideas on practice organization. No specific drills will be explained. Coaches desiring specific drills for developing any defensive technique would do well to consult Coaches Choice Books and Videos, which is *the* source for obtaining the most comprehensive and detailed information on the subject of defensive drills.

Organize practice schedules into blocks of time. Not every block will be used every day, and the amount of time devoted to each block will vary depending upon need. Chart 14-1 illustrates a block in which specific individual techniques are developed. Charts 14-2 through 14-6 illustrate blocks in which the coordination of group skills are developed.

POSITIONS	ACTIVITY TYPE: Individual
Nose and Ends	Emphasize defensive skills versus the run: • Movement drills that develop agility, quickness, balance, coordination, and intense effort. • Tackling drills from different angles. • Drills that teach the fundamentals of defeating a 1-on-1 run block (hook, drive, kick-out, trap, etc. • Drills that teach the fundamentals of defeating 2-on-1 run blocks (kiss, fold, zone, double team, etc).
Tandems	Emphasize defensive skills versus the run: • Movement drills that develop agility, quickness, balance, coordination, and intense effort. • Tackling drills from different angles. • One-on-one drills (versus linemen and running backs) that emphasize defeating and shedding blockers.
Stud/Rover	Emphasize defensive skills versus the run: • Movement drills that develop agility, quickness, balance, coordination, and intense effort. • Tackling drills from different angles. • 1-on-1 drills (versus linemen and running backs).
Corners and Safety	Emphasize defensive skills versus the run: • Crack and replace drills with both linebackers and defensive backs. • Alley support drills for the free safety. • Tackling drills.

Chart 14-1

POSITIONS	ACTIVITY TYPE: Group/Individual
Nose, Ends, and Tandems	Emphasize defensive skills versus the run: • 5-on-6 blocking scheme read drill (backfield can be included). Emphasize zone, iso, trap, veer, and fold.
Stud/Rover	Emphasize man-man coverage skills: • Footwork drills. • Jam and funnel drills. • Ball-catching drills. • Drills that teach the exact body position for covering each pass route that a defender will encounter (out, hook, seam, etc.). • 1-on-1 drills. Stud and Rover versus offensive receivers. • 2-on-2 and 3-on-3 drills that emphasize picks, rubs, wheels, and so forth. • Drills that teach defenders to strip the ball out of a receiver's possession.
Corners and Safety	Emphasize man-man coverage skills: • Footwork drills. • Jam and funnel drills. • Ball-catching drills. • Drills that teach the exact body position for covering each pass route that a defender will encounter (out, curl, fade, comeback, etc.). • 1-on-1 drills. Defensive backs versus offensive receivers. • 2-on-2 and 3-on-3 drills that emphasize picks, rubs, wheels, and so forth. • Drills that teach defenders to strip the ball out of a receiver's possession.

Chart 14-2

POSITIONS	ACTIVITY TYPE: Group/Individual
Nose, Ends, and Tandems	Emphasize defensive skills versus pass and run: • 5-on-6 blocking scheme read drill (backfield can be included). Emphasize inside counter trey, weakside sweep and speed option from ace, zone and pass.
Stud/Rover	Emphasize zone coverage skills: • Drops. • Quarterback and pattern reads. • Playing specific pass route combinations.
Corners and Safety	Emphasize zone coverage skills: • Coverage techniques (backpedal, jam, etc.). • Quarterback and pattern reads. • Playing specific pass route combinations.

Chart 14-3

POSITIONS	ACTIVITY TYPE: Group/Individual
Nose and Ends	Emphasize pass rush techniques: • Techniques (rip, swim, etc.). • Pass rush lanes.
Linebackers and Defensive Backs	Emphasize one-on-one versus offensive receivers: • Defenders will employ man-to-man techniques versus various individual receivers.

Chart 14-4

POSITIONS	ACTIVITY TYPE: Group/Individual
Nose, Ends, and Tandems	Emphasize defensive skills versus run and pass: • 5-on-6 blocking scheme read drill (backfield can be included). • Emphasize inside counter trey, weakside sweep and speed option from aceback backfield, zone and pass.
Stud/Rover	Emphasize zone coverage skills: • Pattern reads.

Chart 14-5

POSITIONS	ACTIVITY TYPE: Group
Nose, Ends, and Tandems	3-on-5 drill: • Defensive line will work pass rush techniques versus five offensive linemen.
Linebackers and Defensive Backs	6-on-8 drill: • Eight defenders will employ a variety of coverages versus a quarterback and five receivers.

Chart 14-6

In addition to the individual and group blocks, schedule team blocks to include the following:

- Team pursuit drills.
- Option defensive drills. Practice time should be devoted to defending the option each and every week, even if your opponent is not an option team. Coaches frequently say that their team was "beaten by an option team" because it was impossible to prepare their defense for this style of offense in one week. This statement is quite true, and because you never want to go into a game unprepared, it is vital to practice against the option at least once or twice a week.
- Team adjustment period versus a multitude of offensive formations, motions, shifts, and so forth. Use five barrels to represent the offensive line, and a quarterback and five offensive players to represent the backs and receivers. This quick, high-rep activity forces the defense line up quickly. Include stunts in this activity and make the appropriate check-offs.
- Team tag versus a scout team. Live scrimmage is seldom engaged during the season. Have a scout team run the opponent's offense versus the defense. The defenders will pursue the ball and tag the ballcarrier. Although the tempo of this drill is full speed, never allow cut blocks or tackling. This approach increases play recognition and reduces the risk of injuries.
- Restrict live scrimmage to spring ball and during the preseason.

About the Authors

Leo Hand assumed the position of the defensive backfield coach at Andress High School in 2004. Hand previously served as the defensive coordinator at El Paso (Texas) High School from 2001 to 2003. Prior to that, he held the same position with Irvin High School in El Paso, Texas. With over 36 years of experience as a teacher and coach, Hand has served in a variety of coaching positions in his career—achieving a notable level of success at each stop.

A graduate of Emporia State University in Emporia, Kansas, Hand began his football-coaching career in 1968 as the junior varsity coach for McQuaid Jesuit High School in Rochester, New York. After two seasons, Hand accepted the job as the offensive line coach at Aquinas Institute (1970-1971), and then served as the head coach at Saint John Fisher College for two years. Hand has also served on the gridiron staffs at APW (Parrish, NY) High School (head coach); Saint Anthony (Long Beach, CA) High School (head coach), Daniel Murphy (Los Angeles, CA) High School (head coach), Servite (Anaheim, CA) High School (head coach); Serra (Gardena, CA) High School (head coach); Long Beach (CA) City College (offensive line and linebackers); and Los Angeles (CA) Harbor College (offensive coordinator).

During the last six years that he spent coaching interscholastic teams in California, Hand's squads won 81 percent of their games in the highly competitive area of Southern California. At Serra High School, his teams compiled a 24-1 record, won a CIF championship, and were declared California State champions. On numerous occasions, Hand has helped rebuild several floundering gridiron teams into highly successful programs. Hand has been honored on numerous occasions with Coach of the Year recognition for his efforts.

A former Golden Gloves boxing champion, Hand is a prolific author. He has written several football instructional books and published numerous articles. With his wife Mary, Hand has nine children and 11 grandchildren.

Rick Molina is the defensive backfield coach at El Dorado High School in El Paso, Texas. Upon graduation from Burges High School (Texas) in 1995, Molina attended The University of Texas at El Paso, where he played as a walk-on for the Miners' football team. In 1997, UTEP awarded him a full scholarship for his gridiron efforts. A two-year letterman at UTEP, Molina started two years on special teams, and played free safety and cornerback. A 2000 graduate with a degree in criminal justice, Molina began his coaching career as a volunteer assistant coach, working with the secondary at his high school alma mater. He then accepted a full-time assistant's position at El Paso High School, where he worked with the secondary and special teams (2002-2003). Rick and his wife, Christin, have two children, Tyler and Dezerae.